"THE PROBLEM WITH BLACK PEOPLE"

A collection of writings on race, identity and systemic oppression

ANGELO C. LOUW

First published in South Africa with Special Permission from the Author by AfroStory (Pty) Ltd.

Special thanks to The Daily Maverick, The Daily Vox, News 24, Sunday Times, and others acknowledged. Assembled by Angelo C Louw.

PRAISE FOR THE AUTHOR

"Angelo Louw is a talented, powerful filmmaker and I'm excited about the release of his collection of essays. Louw's voice is thoughtful, impassioned and unapologetic in its call for justice, fairness and accountability. This is a collection to read, heed and learn from."

— YEWANDE OMOTOSO, AWARD-WINNING NOVELIST

"Angelo has created and displayed a wealth of positive queer narrative that seeks to improve the lives of others, particularly Queer people. Angelo's ability to interpret and critique the toxicity of structures that are homophobic and transphobic, and bring about change including addressing the intersections of it."

— MMAPASEKA STEVE LETSIKE, HUMAN RIGHTS ADVOCATE

CONTENTS

DEDICATION

To my mother, her mother, and all our mothers
burdened with the weight of the world.

COLOURED, COLOURISM AND PRIVILEGE

Chapter 1

As a child, I absolutely dreaded bath time. It may seem a trivial fact, but my disposition to daily grooming extended far beyond mere disappointment about an abrupt end to playtime…

Bath time, for me, meant my grandmother shouting for one of my four older cousins to fetch the orange net bag and ammonia floor cleaner from under the sink, so that she could scrub the black off my neck.

The mixing of enslaved populations in the Cape transferred traits from many other ethnic groups to Khoi-San people – traits such as skin pigmentation from the Indians; a trait that I am prone to. It's genetic – but my grandmother would scrub the colour off my skin with chemical-based household cleaner like dirt. And although physically painful, what hurt most was the sound of my cousins sniggering at the ridiculousness of the situation from the other side of the door.

I carried this trauma with me for most of my adolescence. I bought into my grandmother's association of pigmentation to dirt, and even adopted her torture in order to prevent any further embarrassment. I tried everything from toothpaste to complexion creams – and even ventured into other household cleaners like green Sunlight soap.

My grandmother's mission to keep the fairest of her children's complexion as white as a porcelain doll is a type of madness that seems absolutely irrational and inhumane on the surface; but, it was rooted in a longstanding heritage of assimilation to whiteness as a ticket to privilege in the Coloured community.

In her memoir, *The Keeper of Kumm*, Sylvia Vollenhoven recalls her formative years in which being classified "mixed" afforded her family the ability to live "next to the school for the fair kids of the Coloured middle-classes" but not the esteem of those she calls "less mixed".

She writes that being called the k-word was at the top of the list of insults for dark-skinned Coloured kids.

"It is right up there alongside *Boesman* or *Hotnot*. Name-calling I rail against all through my childhood," she writes.

The anti-apartheid journalist goes in great depth about her own identity politics and experiences of colourism. She describes how she would secretly use her mother's skin lightening creams and straighten her hair just to fit in, to be respected.

But, not even a lifetime of skin-based discrimination could prepare her for the ultimate reminder of the "blackness from which (she had) been running"; the day she received her green government identity card:

"Coloured is just an uncomfortable reality, a place on the margins," she writes. "Other Coloured is the no man's land on the edge of the tenuous border."

In his comparative study of the South Africa Coloured community and the creole population of Louisiana, United States, Dr Blair Proctor noted a natural resentment which occurs in multi-ethnic oppressed groups, where particular groups benefited because of skin colour.

"Specifically, color (sic) determined economic, educational, and political privileges and opportunities for advancement," he writes. "For example, pencil tests and paper bag tests and other forms of tactics were used to determine who was an insider or outsider."

This promise of privilege has had a profound effect, not just on the psyche of Coloured people, but society at large.

While aspirations of whiteness in the community have developed into a culture of body manipulation – evident in the widespread practice of hair straightening – privilege is still safeguarded for those more closely assimilated to whiteness.

International studies show that among people of African descent, there is a clear bias toward those of a lighter complexion, as far as job recruitment is concerned. A Villanova University study found that interviewers deemed lighter-skinned Black people more intelligent than darker-skinned people who had identical credentials.

Closer to home, a recent study found that people who talked with a twang were deemed more trustworthy. The University of Cape Town researchers who conducted the study speculated that those who boosted a "model C" accent were perceived as having a higher social status.

What this means for Coloured South Africans, even in the era of reformative policies such as broad-based black economic empowerment, is the perpetuation of an apartheid social hierarchy – which is clearly evident in the amplified disparities between these communities formed on proximity to whiteness.

Indeed, my grandmother may have suffered a certain type of psychosis when trying to scrub the black off my skin; however, this type of crazy is not limited to her, her posterities or the broader Coloured community, for that matter. It is a mental conditioning that cuts across the social divide.

As Frantz Fanon noted in his 1952 critic of the African diaspora in the United States:

"The colonized (sic) is elevated above his jungle status in proportion to his adoption of the mother country's cultural standards."

DAILY MAVERICK (2018)

STATE HAS RELINQUISHED ITS DUTY OF UPLIFTMENT

Chapter 2

I was taken aback when Pravin Gordhan insinuated that citizens should stop relying on the state for support. He said the state was under too much strain due to growing debt to continue funding projects like housing. It was the responsibility of citizens to develop a culture of entrepreneurship in order to curb reliance on government programmes and grants. It is here that Gordhan erred: we, the people, must take responsibility by playing our role in the development of our country... but so too must the government.

Our research team is analysing trends in budget allocations over the past 10 years and is finding correlations between a stagnant budget for service delivery and an increasing budget for government debt.

For example, while the allocations for general public services and debt service costs were similar in 2010-11 at R60.8-billion and R66.2billion respectively, by 2016-17 they had diverged to

R86.2-billion and R147.7-billion a year.

A perusal of our recent reports illustrates a snowball effect between the mismanagement of government funds and reliance on state funding.

One example is the over- and under-expenditure reported by six provinces relating to the education infrastructure grant over the past two financial years. Therefore, Gordhan's call for the masses to play their part in the financial stability of our country is not only superficial, but highly unfair.

Of course, the public has a role to play in governance beyond voting. Public participation in our nation's affairs is promoted by our constitution, which provides several means for citizens to have their voices heard. But the public entrusts leadership with the responsibility of devising and administering development strategies in the best interests of the larger populace.

What we have witnessed in recent years, however, is a concerted effort to protect failing leaders (selected by struggle credentials rather than merit) at the expense of the accountable, effective governance required by our constitution.

Have our leaders become too comfortable in their positions of power that they are detached from the realities of our country, where 16.3 million South Africans live below the poverty line and 50% of those in work earn poverty wages?

Like Gordhan in his budget speech, President Jacob Zuma made constant reference to his consultations with business in preparation for his state of the nation address. For weeks before these important speeches, commentators across mainstream media called for a "business-friendly" budget.

In all these debates, the constitutional imperative of ensuring an end to poverty and inequality and the enjoyment of fundamental human rights by all was lost.

For an interpretation of why and how this happened one can do worse than read Karl Marx's description of the development of a "petty bourgeoisie" in advanced capitalist societies. That is, a middle class of people so desperate to secure their wealth and status that they will act as a buffer between the underprivileged and the moneyed elite.

Our report on the progressive realisation of the right to food found that while we produce enough food to comfortably feed the nation, half the population suffers from malnourishment — living on cheap, processed foods that are high in sugar and fat. This affects healthcare expenditure due to a rise in dietary related illnesses like diabetes.

It is facts like these that Gordhan fails to mention when he speaks.

SUNDAY TIMES (2016)

TBO TOUCH: TAKING SWIPES AT MOST VULNERABLE WON'T END POVERTY

Chapter 3

"The only difference between the guy I just drove past begging in the street and myself is our mental disposition. Let's change how we THINK."
– Radio personality Thabo "Tbo Touch" Molefe tweeted July 18.

Molefe's assault on the poor is not the first I heard last week; on Monday SAfm hosted a debate chaired by Ashraf Garda about whether or not poverty was just a state of mind, with Former President of the Black Management Forum Buyani Zwane arguing that because he and close friends attained success by working hard and sacrificing time to read at a local Soweto library, there was nothing stopping unemployed youth from doing the same.

SADC Basic Income Grant Campaign Coordinator Vuyokazi Futshane's response quickly, and rightfully, shot down his feel-good anecdote dressed as a solution to youth unemployment in South Africa: "How is a someone from a little rural village in the Eastern Cape, where there are no libraries, going to do that?"

In that statement lies the real cause of poverty in our country: structural inequality so deeply ingrained in the fabric of society that poor South Africans have no real chance to escape it. School infrastructure in rural areas and townships were systematically under-funded during apartheid rule, and remain well below standard. Exorbitant fees deny children from these localities access to good public schools, perpetuating class divisions.

It is these class divisions that have corrupted the likes of Molefe and Zwane into thinking upward mobility rests solely on one's mental disposition. Surrounded by first-world comfort in lush suburbs, it is easy for the middle class (which makes up just under 15% of the total population) to disengage from the lived realities of over half of South Africans, which survives on under R779 a month.

The fact of the matter is that many South Africans are but a pay cheque away from poverty; 20% of the population fell beneath the poverty line after the 2009 recession. When your main concern is ensuring that your family has something to eat at night or when all you can focus on is your hunger pains, it isn't very easy to think about anything else. We are not talking about a bunch of MacBook wielding, Starbucks free Wi-Fi using "consultants" when we talk about the poor.

"Some entrepreneur from Diepsloot is going to open a business thats [sic] going to hire ppl [sic] from Sandton. Your mind is a powerful weapon," Molefe tweeted the day after his ignorance went viral.

So skewed is Molefe's understanding of class in South Africa, he seems to believe the measure to success is to invert an apartheid hierarchy where a poor Black person can be the boss of white people, and not the amount of jobs they can create for the community they are from – mind you, two in every five Black South Africans are unemployed. His logic only stands to further deepen class divisions in South Africa, which are practically determined by race.

I find it heinous to place the burden of ending poverty in the hands of the poor when class disparity is a deliberate project to create a flow of cheap labour to grow South Africa's economy. This system is strong and damning for a majority of those living in the country. I don't see why it never crosses our minds to bring those responsible for this poverty to account?

Why aren't we upping taxes on the extractives industry to fund better social protection projects in South Africa? Heck, the continent loses $60 billion in illicit cash flows per year. It's about time we implemented a national minimum wage, despite scare tactics by big business; more money in the hands of the South African workforce simulates the economy, creates new jobs and stability in our country.

The solution to inequality lies solely in the hands of those with actual power to make necessary and impactful changes. Perhaps Molefe was right about people needing to think differently, after all; he was just not speaking to or about the right people.

NEWS24 (2017)

EXPLOITATION IS 'DRIVING' XENOPHOBIA IN CAPE TOWN

Escalating xenophobia in South Africa is tarnishing its "Rainbow Nation". But over the past year, the spotlight has increasingly shifted focus to Cape Town because of a series of events culminating in the Greenmarket Square sit-in — in which hundreds of foreign nationals demanded the South African find them asylum in safer countries — and the subsequent forced relocation of those involved.

By 2018, South Africa hosted more than 270,000 refugees and asylum seekers, of whom 84% come from sub-Saharan Africa. Many of these foreign nationals came here to escape poverty, political violence and war. But in recent years, conditions in the country have become equally as dangerous to them because of sporadic Afrophobic violence, dressed as xenophobic attacks.

Ours is a country experiencing grave poverty and one of the world's highest unemployment rates, and rhetoric would have you believe that foreign nationals are responsible for it. But the true culprits are businesses exploiting the vulnerability of undocumented immigrants living in our country, to bypass the labour laws protecting legal labour in South Africa, our citizens and others permitted to work here.

Upon visiting Cape Town to produce *"GUTTED"*, I began recording conversations with Uber drivers, mostly from Zimbabwe. I had no particular ambition for these recordings, I just found our chats to be incredibly insightful. But upon review, what I found was a recurring narrative about work, the ability to work and vulnerability caused by its necessity.

Talent's case is one such example of the types of abuse foreign nationals have to endure due to the vulnerability of being undocumented in South Africa. The Zimbabwean immigrant, who drove me to the airport early one morning, had uprooted his family because of his job, a manager of one of Johannesburg's top restaurants, when they decided to expand into Cape Town. Just over a year had passed and he found himself out of work, becoming a driver to support his family.

"I didn't like being in the fridge all day, and my doctor advised me against it," he said. "I was always getting sick. [It was the] same problem all the time. So he told me at some point the drugs will stop working and I won't have anything to help me. Those antibiotics are not meant for prolonged periods."

When Talent informed his bosses about the health issues he had developed at the new restaurant, he was met with indifference. He believes his managers' lack of empathy was rooted in racism, having observed a very different experience when his white colleagues had fallen ill.

Trymore, an Uber Black driver who accepted my regular ride request so that he wouldn't waste a trip back to town, told me that the possibility of experiencing racism is one of the biggest reasons a lot of his South African friends refused to become Uber drivers. He thought this logic was ludicrous given the amount of unemployment in the country. He had never experienced anything like that as an Uber driver; in fact, it helped him get the luxury vehicle he was coining it with.

"I asked them, 'Why don't you guys just come to Uber?'," he said. "They say, '*Hawu kanti…* I can't drive white people. Every time, they want you to call them: boss, boss, boss'."

However, I had the chance to engage a South African Uber driver named Anees on the matter while he drove me to Canal Walk one evening. He added another dimension to the debate. He said that local cab drivers did not want to join Uber, despite its popularity, because many of them currently work for companies which provided vehicles, whereas if they became Uber drivers, they would have to rent a vehicle for as much as R2,500 per week.

"They don't want to work with that pressure. With meter cabs, if I don't make money, the boss won't make money," he said. "So for instance, they will drive for R10 per kilometre: R5 will go to the boss and R5 for them. So, if I don't do a trip, I don't owe the boss anything. So he can sit there and he can sleep the whole day."

But, cab drivers have not taken lightly to this disruption to their job security and have attempted to intimidate Uber drivers ever since the service first became available in the country. Anees said that the fact that he was South African protected him from these attacks; in fact, cab drivers were intentionally preying on the vulnerability of foreign nationals driving for the service.

"A lot of these guys that are threatening people are also just trying their luck. They judge you by your appearance," he said. "So, I look like a local... so, I can equally retaliate the same way that they are treating me, whereas these foreigners are too scared to get into trouble because half of them are not here legally."

Eden, a driver with whom I found myself weaving through Woodstock's side roads during traffic, said that foreign nationals driving for Uber were even easy targets for the city, which has a backlog of permit request spanning years.

"A quick notification that this is an Uber is if you are carrying a white person, and I'm black," he said. "Even the police, they give us a hard time now, they are impounding cars. So, it's quick for them to tell that it is an Uber, especially if you are carrying a white person. It's a big disaster."

He said that his friends have even resorted to asking their passengers to drive through roadblocks so that they do not lose their cars because the police do not mess with white drivers. For those who are not so lucky, they've had to pay fines up to R14,000 depending on the number of times they have been impounded for being caught without the permits they so patiently wait for.

Living under the constant threat to the lives they have built has left countless asylum seekers in the city at the mercy of everyone looking to save or make a quick buck. Xenophobia violence may be sporadic in nature, but foreign nationals living in South Africa are under constant attack. Theirs is a daily battle in which they have no choice but to watch their human dignity being stripped away bit by bit.

THE DAILY VOX (2020)

JUMPING THROUGH HOOPS FOR WHITE PEOPLE'S CHANGE

Chapter 5

Is it just me or is Johannesburg North turning into one big circus? Pantsula dancers, jugglers on unicycles and clowns – well, men dressed as clowns minus the routine – all trying to make a quick buck while traffic moves at the pace of a mall parking lot on the weekend.

"Well, at least they are not asking for a handout," I've heard people say, but that it has got to a point where Black people literally have to jump through hoops for bread and milk money is about as funny as these so-called clowns (...not at all!).

Have we become so immune to Black suffering that we easily gaze over it if it doesn't come knocking on our window, juggling balls with one hand?

The fact that poverty among Black people has become normalised to a point where we are no longer triggered by it, speaks volumes about where we expect black South Africans to sit in the social order – and there you were thinking apartheid was dead and gone, when it's done is found a cozy nook in your mind to fester in.

How did this become a race thing? You may ask. Black people aren't the only ones that are poor, right? Well, I certainly don't see any white youth out there putting on a full-on show for your pocket change. Do you?

Because if these were white kids, you'd hear about it on the news, someone in the world would crowdsource funding for them to go to university, and these talented individuals would end up in a TV ad or two, launching illustrious entertainment careers.

Let's face it, suburbanites are more likely to give their spare coins (paper money even) to model C school-goers begging for cash to visit Switzerland over the July break than black mothers who are trying to feed their children, because:

"How can they keep those kids out of school like that? Shame man. We mustn't encourage these women by giving them money."

Forget that the fact that they can barely afford to feed these kids, let alone bus them to school every morning at the risk of missing peak hour traffic; the racist undertone of this sort of thinking places the onus on unemployed Black women who have fallen into a vicious cycle of poverty that is structural, widespread and proven by scientific research.

Stereotypes of lazy Black people, Black entitlement and Black hypersexuality are at play here – and we all know that stereotypes play an important part in the preservation of power systems, as they create negative stigma around certain groups, making others more desirable.

Don't get me wrong, public performance is not unique to Joburg; all over the world, people put on shows for tourists: Elvis impersonators on the Las Vegas strip, Masai warriors ready for photo ops at Kenyan markets.

The difference, however, is that these are not our tourism districts and these kids aren't performing to foreigners with pockets full of spending money; the only thing separating them and their audience is a 20km or so commute.

It is perverse that any South African needs to shuck and jive for the entertainment of another in order to make five bucks per traffic light change. Dancing in the heat all day, dressed in thick pantsula overalls, face painted like a clown... all so that wealthy children strapped into overpriced car seats can clap along in the rear-view mirror as mommy searches her ashtray for loose change.

Youth unemployment and lack of access to development opportunities is forcing young Black South Africans into spectacle for the humour of wealthy suburbanites, and boy do they enjoy a good show! You ever been to an orphanage when funders visit and see those kids break out into *Sarafina*-type song – Colgate smiles and jazz hands? Performances so memorable they stay top of mind during funding renewal cycles.

The gap between the haves and have-nots is mind-boggling for a country so rich in natural resources. Levels of inequality are so high that only 16 people (let me spell it out: *s-i-x-t-e-e-n* people) own the same exact amount of wealth as half of the population – that's over 26 million South Africans!

The worst part of it is that those at the bottom of the spectrum are the ones indigenous to this bountiful land. And as they continue to plummet into hopelessness, as national poverty trends demonstrate, they become more and more vulnerable to the worst type of humiliation.

So while many marvel at the performers who turn traffic lights into their ring curbs, I see a vile display of inequality in South Africa, a Cirque du Soleil of poverty.

THE DAILY VOX (2019)

WOKE AND #ONFLEEK IN AMERICA

Chapter 6

"**I**'m a vers queer, gender neutral, intersectional feminist who believes that masc, fem, gay, black, women, immigrants, trans and everything in-between have a right to love and be loved! LABELS DON'T DEFINE US, OUR HUMILITY DOES! If you don't get it, ask me about it or move on."
— From a new friend's bio on Jack'd.

While hanging out with this particular friend, he seemed very confused by the fact that I am from a country called South Africa because he thought Africa was a country and not a continent; it was also a surprise to him that the United States was, in fact, a country and not a continent.

"Is Canada a continent?" he asked, to which I replied, "No, Canada and the US are both on a continent called North America." (#MindBlown)

I didn't want to insult his intelligence; heaven knows, he seemed to be on a quest for knowledge and truth, and more importantly, justice — "woke," in short. I failed to understand, however, how someone could throw around big concepts like "intersectional feminist" on social media, but lack pretty basic geographical knowledge, especially about the country of their birth.

I am not saying that my buddy doesn't actually grasp the difference between "white privilege" and "racial supremacy," but it is really a statement of the times we live in when being woke is #OnFleek and youth are able to (fairly) critique "transracialism" in blog posts faster than recalling the name of Rihanna's current chart position.

"Oppressed people cannot remain oppressed forever. The yearning for freedom eventually manifests itself, and that is what has happened to the American Negro. Something within has reminded him of his birthright of freedom, and something without has reminded him that it can be gained."

— Rev Martin Luther King Jr
from a Birmingham jail in 1963.

In the wake of the 40th Anniversary of King's assassination, I stumbled on this paragraph from a letter he wrote reflecting on the social climate leading to the civil rights protests of the 1960s — on Facebook, of course. He suggested that revolt was inevitable, natural even: an effect of atrocities caused to a suffering people.

This gave me a new perspective on the so-called trend of "wokeness": It is the "yearning for freedom" that King speaks of manifesting itself.

In recent months, I've had the privilege to engage several civil rights movement leaders on the current political climate, including King's right-hand man, Bernard LaFayette Jr. All of them seem wary about this new wave of pro-black protest — particularly the efforts of #BlackLivesMatter. Their main criticism is that these movements lack foresight.

Black Panthers Founder Bobby Seale said at a Washington DC discussion of his new book last October: "I am a programmes person; I don't care too much for over-intellectualising. ... I want to see Black Lives Matter initiate job programs and feeding schemes."

While I couldn't agree more that job programs and feeding schemes are necessary and will assist marginalised communities in the United States, I don't believe that the impact of such movements is as trivial as many seem to think.

In this climate of pro-black advocacy, we've witnessed a substantial decrease in the sale of hair relaxer, plans for reform in a racially biased criminal justice system and a conviction that paves the way for hate speech criminalisation — that is, the case of the white Georgia couple who were criminally charged for waving a Confederate flag and shotgun at a Black child's birthday party.

It's a shame that my new friend, as a product of an inferior education system, is not able to distinguish between certain countries and continents, but I am enthused by his thoughts on intersectionality and feminism. His calls of social justice have not gone ignored, evidently. In fact, his protest might just lead to a better education for future generations of marginalised youth.

While there may not be a concrete plan in place for feeding the underprivileged and housing the homeless, these continued public calls for justice might just lead to such grand schemes. I mean, they have certainly got us talking about it: #BlackLivesMatter has appeared on Twitter 12 million times so far.

As African-American nationalist and civil rights movement leader Malcolm X put it:

"The greatest mistake of the movement has been trying to organise a sleeping people around specific goals. You have to wake the people up first, then you'll get action."

THE BALTIMORE SUN (2017)

EDUCATION APARTHEID WEAKENS 'POWERFUL WEAPON' FOR CHANGE

Chapter 7

"**E**ducation is the most powerful weapon which you can use to change the world."

— Nelson Mandela.

The degrees on my wall have opened up the world to me, a township boy who would otherwise be working in customer service. I write this today a stone's throw away from Washington DC, where I reside upon invitation by the US State Department. I write this to achieve change in my country. So, perhaps the father of our nation was right.

A few weeks ago, students from various universities in New York marched to the South African consulate to hand over a letter of demands to Mninwa Johannes Mahlangu, our ambassador to the US. The march, in solidarity with #FeesMustFall protestors, called for free primary, secondary and tertiary education funded by a wealth tax.

Since last year, South African students have led this campaign for free tertiary education, as escalated fees have caused many poor, predominantly Black, South Africans to face financial exclusion from institutions of higher learning, damning them to a life of poverty.

However, this has not been an easy fight, nor has it proved to be very fruitful – despite getting the presidency to commit to a "special task team" exploring better funding mechanisms. An entire year has passed since then with no change at universities such as the University of Witwatersrand, Johannesburg, which recently made international headlines due to police violence.

I find it disturbing that I can just re-post content featured on Facebook memories from a year back that is still relevant today. But, as I scroll down my timeline, the images I see don't just remind me of the spectacular protests mobilised by student leaders last year, they remind of the times we protested at that very university about this very issue almost ten years ago – rubber bullets and all.

These protests are nothing new, nor was the university's violent response to them. What has changed is that this generation of students is brave enough to face the bullets fired at them and retaliate with the brick and stone at their disposal.

In the space of just eight years, courses I attended and struggled to afford have quadrupled in cost. So, perhaps it is despair and not bravery compelling academia to militancy.

"Are we so immersed in this terror narrative, like [Johnathan] Jansen, that we don't see how systems of oppression create monsters?" asked South African columnist Azad Essa after media criticised #FeesMustFall protestors for setting alight a University of KwaZulu-Natal library.

Just two years ago, at the release of its 2013 General Household Survey, Statistics SA's Statistician General Pali Lehohla called for an increase in the number of Black students attending university to improve economic development.

The report found only 3.2 percent of Black youth aged between 18 and 29 attended university that year, while white attendance in the same demographic was 18.7 percent. This is not surprising, because an earlier Statistics SA report found 54 percent of Black South Africans live below the poverty line, while poverty only affects less than one percent of all White South Africans. Financial exclusion only deepens this divide.

When the #FeesMustFall movement first gained traction last year, Director of the Centre for Education Rights and Transformation Salim Vally reported to the media that free education for the poor was viable in South Africa as per the study his team conducted for our department of higher education in 2012.

Last month, Vally and a team of education specialists, again, pointed out our government's gross underfunding of the sector in an *Independent Online* op-ed. "South Africa's state budget for universities as a percentage of GDP. is 0.75%. The Africa-wide average is 0.78%; the proportion of GDP for Senegal and Ghana is 1.4% and Cuba 4.5%," they wrote.

However, their pleas to the government appear to fall on deaf ears. The problem, it seems, has nothing to do with a so-called lack of resources, but an unwillingness to change the status quo. Are they threatened by the influence of these student leaders, and hogging power because they are not done looting? They turn us into criminals when we get in the way of their thuggery.

I have watched YouTube videos of police opening fire on students gathered outside the university's most iconic building melancholically singing "*Asina'mali* [We don't have money]."

Media For Justice, a social justice investigative unit, documented several stories of students being shot at in their dormitory rooms for having their lights on after curfew.

Just a few weeks ago, a student leader was shot thirteen times in the back, at a very close range in a targeted attack on students. This just after addressing the police and turning to speak to the crowd.

"I have heard of other comrades assisting an injured student and being told by the police to leave her or face being shot at by rubber bullet," Shaeera Khalla wrote on Facebook hours later. "In extreme pain in the emergency section of the hospital; I was greeted by three policemen, who demanded I provide them with a statement."

When news about the ambush broke, spokesperson of opposition party, Economic Freedom Fighters, tweeted that over 600 students have been detained to date, as well as lecturers from the University of KwaZulu-Natal for engaging students on their concerns.

These narratives of governmental terror sound all too familiar to me. They are reminiscent of those you are likely to read about in textbooks documenting our apartheid history; the same books that we have studied from. However, a closer look at those textbooks will show you that not even apartheid could match the tenacity of South African youth.

NNPA NEWSWIRE (2016)

DO LEARNERSHIPS PERPETUATE BLACK-WHITE EARNINGS GAP?

Chapter 8

It is a bitter pill to swallow that so many years after apartheid there exists such a huge gap in the average monthly earnings between black and white professionals in South Africa. According to earnings monitoring firm Analytico, white professionals earn almost three times higher than their Black counterparts: R20,000 and R8,000 respectively.

A string of reports by Statistics South Africa (Stats SA) highlight alarming disparities between races at all levels of society, which continue to grow. These reports demonstrate how population groups indigenous to South Africa remain in a downward spiral because they continue to face the host of structural drivers of inequality.

Last year, reflecting on findings of one such report, Statistician

General Pali Lehohla warned that South Africa faced a "cocktail of disasters" as their report noted that Black and Coloured youth experienced unemployment at a disproportionate rate, correlating with poor levels of higher education attainment in both population groups.

The report, which assessed the vulnerability of South African youth, found that youth unemployment was strongly linked to those who have not completed matric, with 57% without a job, compared to an unemployment rate of 38% among those who completed matric. It also found the employability increased with higher levels of education.

Lehohla has since stressed that tertiary education is key in tackling unemployment in South Africa, as young people obtain specialised skills at institutions of higher learning that not only increase the likelihood of finding employment, but their market value too.

However, recent research by Studies in Poverty and Inequality Institute shows that while unemployment levels experienced between those without matric far outweighs that of university graduates, the number of unemployed people who have a tertiary education has increased by more than 150% since 2008.

Government incentivised programmes, such as corporate learnerships, aim to achieve New Growth Path goals of restructuring the South African economy to improve its performance in terms of labour absorption, composition and growth rate.

While collaborative efforts between government and business to curb unemployment seems like a win-win situation, low wage benchmarks set by the Department of Labour have lasting consequences for workplace entrants enrolled in such schemes.

International studies show that earnings received in the beginning of a worker's career have a profound impact on the trajectory of income growth over the course of their life. A report by the Federal Reserve Bank of New York analysing the career paths of 5 million people found that workers could expect a 38% pay swell by the end of their careers.

Current learnership allowances are set at around R3,500 per month for persons with a degree; that is over two times less than the national average starting salary for persons with a bachelor's degree – which sits at R8,270, according to Analytico.

It is, then, not surprising that there exists this huge pay gap, since those professionals starting out on learnerships are so poorly valued at the onset of their career, as compared to their fairer counterparts who have an easier time walking into jobs after university, according to SA private sector employment trends.

While there exists no data to verify this, the absence of such data makes it very difficult to dismiss either. In fact, the absence of any kind of monitoring makes it very hard to gauge the exact social impact of such schemes – positive or negative.

Yes, learnerships are an entry point for many Black professionals into corporate SA. But, how easily businesses are able to create positions for Black graduates when promised tax breaks, shows that demand is there, just not the will.

That business is only ready to employ Black labour at a discounted rate, clearly demonstrates the need for transformation these programmes aim to achieve; however, perpetuating wage inequality in order to do so is counterproductive, especially looking at the negative impact low wages have on deepening poverty.

If business is genuinely interested in transformation, a good starting point is to pay employees fairly. Even if learnership doesn't count as formal employment, enrolled graduates contribute to a business like any newly qualified employee would; they deserve reasonable reimbursement. Anything less is superficial and contributes to the problem.

HUFFINGTON POST (2018)

THE MATH (AND SCIENCE) BEHIND BLACK TAX

Chapter 9

Every year, without fail - and I am tempted to say since the dawn of our democracy, when people of colour began entering the professional workforce - a very uncomfortable debate flares up in the workplace when offices reopen after the festive season.

The social phenomenon that is "Black tax" is almost always shut down as "race card" rhetoric, but a look at socioeconomic trends in the country will finally give Black and brown professionals the scientific leg to stand on when putting forward their argument.

The usual scenario: our white colleagues show off their newly acquired tans and Instagram pictures from exotic travel destinations (Bali, Barcelona... basically any place from the Flight Centre special catalog with good weather). Sipho stumbles into the office halfway through John's account of his life-changing elephant ride and laments how he wishes he, too, could visit an exotic island one day - after relaying his festive season salutations to his fellow colleagues, of course.

JOHN: Why can't you? You can get a package for next to nothing.

SIPHO: I have too many responsibilities; you know, *Black tax.*

JOHN: Ag, rubbish. We all help our families out from time to time.

While it is true that most people have to help their families out, others have to help their families out a little more than "from time to time". And, this seems to be the point of contention; sometimes it is hard to perceive other people's point of view, especially when you seemingly have the same lived experience.

John and Sipho may work in the same company, they may even earn the same salary, and they may very well "help out" at home; but, chances are that Sipho is helping out on a far more regular basis than his colleague... Black tax is a matter of scale.

Here is the science: Sipho is Black. John is white. Poverty levels between these population groups are highly skewed. Statistics SA have documented that over 50% of Black people in our country live below the poverty line, as compared to less than 1% of white people. Already, there is less of a financial strain on white people to keep their community afloat.

Now, some may argue that neither Sipho nor John, based on their earning potential in the professional work environment, are likely to be considered below the poverty line. True. However, Sipho's likelihood of coming from a poorer household is certainly increased, to say the least, by the trends mentioned above. So, when you apply that to the University of Witwatersrand's research on the national minimum wage, you will see that "Black tax" isn't just an excuse to get out of after work drinks.

Their studies show that the average worker from a poor household supports two and a half other people, as compared to the average worker from a middle-class household who only supports one other person. That's the difference, John. It's a one and half person difference; or in scientific terms, it's a 150% difference. Black tax is the 150% more that people of colour, particularly Black people, have to contribute toward their households. It is measurable, and therefore, tangible.

This doesn't even account for the student debt that many Black professionals are burdened with, or the multitude of things people of colour would have to acquire just to have a job - clothes, car (yes, some jobs actually require you to have your own vehicle in order to be considered for the position)...

The above equation only speaks to the monthly utility bills we're likely to inherit upon entering the workplace, or the dependents we'd have to add to our medical aid policies. And these are only entry level expenses; when you become a higher income earner, you are expected to chip in a little more at any type of family-related affair. (And all of this, John, on the same salary that you and I both earn). But, I won't go into the specifics; I feel the numbers pretty much speak for themselves.

Black tax has much graver social implications than not being able to splurge on overseas travel and exclusion from social gatherings. The elevated rate in which people of colour have to contribute toward their families' well-being means that they are less likely to be in a position to accumulate wealth, since there is a lot less money left to save; and that means that divide between the have and have-nots will continue to grow (even if the existing earnings gap between the races shrinks).

That, in turn, means that our poverty trends between race

groups are likely to go unchanged - the same poverty trends that perpetuate Black tax in the first place. In short, Black tax is here to stay - well, that is, until we go through some sort of radical economic transformation; but let's face it, South Africa is caught in too strong of an economic headlock for that.

So, while colleagues on the other side of the colour line may share similar hay grades (which, if you don't know, is a measure of superiority in the organisational hierarchy which determines your remuneration or pay) they most probably do not share socioeconomic backgrounds, and will not have a shared financial experience.

Just because John does not pay Black tax, doesn't mean it doesn't exist; it just does not exist to him. Besides, if John did pay it, it wouldn't be called *Black* tax, right? It's simple mathematics.

(2023)

ZERO MINIMUM WAGE EQUALS MAXIMUM SHAME

Chapter 10

The introduction of a national minimum wage is a contentious issue that has been repeatedly delayed by a narrow focus on its potential impact on company bottom lines; but, as long as the country stalls on implementation, it digs itself deeper into despair.

As demonstrated in a 2015 working paper by the National Minimum Wage Research Initiative at the University of the Witwatersrand, the wage gap between poor and non-poor workers reinforces socioeconomic inequality. An analysis of the 2013 National Income Dynamics Study found that the average non-poor earner supports one other person financially whereas poor earners have a higher ratio of 2.65 people. This implies dependents of low-wage workers have little hope of escaping poverty because of limited resources, and that more people are likely to find themselves living below the breadline.

A national minimum wage is not the silver bullet that will

address poverty and inequality in South Africa. It is, however, a proven means of addressing social injustice by closing the inequality gap and a significant step towards achieving a decent living level for all.

Criticism of the minimum wage is fierce, with politicians and business alike raising concerns around the potential negative consequences that they perceive will follow such a shift in policy, particularly layoffs of unskilled labour by businesses to counter the financial implications.

The director of the Free Market Foundation, Jasson Urbach, wrote in a recent *Business Day* opinion piece that "when the price of labour goes up to such an extent, the demand for it will go down". He said that because of this, the most principled case against the minimum wage is that it is "morally wrong". However, such a stance on the proposal is grossly misguided as it is the reluctance of business to invest in the economic wellbeing of their workers that is morally depraved.

That we are still unable to persuade South African business to partner with us in the pursuit of a decent living level for all, nearly a year after negotiations were meant to conclude, is not surprising. Too many business leaders remain guided by an outdated business ethic rooted in our colonial past.

Patrice Lumumba, the first legally elected prime minister of the Democratic Republic of Congo, famously said: "The colonists care nothing for Africa for her own sake. They are attracted by African riches and their actions are guided by the desire to preserve their interests in Africa against the wishes of the African people. For the colonists, all means are good if they help them possess these riches."

We cannot continue to allow business to violate the human rights of the vast majority of people in this country. Deputy

President Cyril Ramaphosa's attempts to sweet-talk business – on the premise that the minimum wage will increase spending power and stimulate economic growth – afford business too much influence over our country's future.

Meanwhile, the long-awaited ratification by the government of the International Covenant on Economic, Social and Cultural Rights in April last year enshrined the right to work in South Africa as well as the right of everyone to just and favourable conditions of work. This includes the requirement that the government take steps to ensure that workers receive fair wages. Countries like Germany have gone as far as to criminalise non-adherence to legislation that guarantees a national minimum wage. What's stopping us implementing similar measures?

On Workers Day, we pay our respects to those who have built our country. Few appreciated their sacrifices more than the former leader of the SACP, Chris Hani, whose words at the ANC Morogoro conference in 1969 continue to resonate.

"Our nationalism must not . . . be confused with the classical drive by an elitist group among the oppressed people to gain ascendancy so they can replace the oppressor in the exploitation of the masses," he said.

"Victory must embrace more than formal political democracy. To allow the existing economic forces to retain their interests intact is to feed the root of racial supremacy and does not represent even the shadow of liberation."

SUNDAY TIMES (2016)

TRUMP AND THE NEW BUSINESS OF POLITICS

Chapter 11

"**I** am more afraid of one hundred sheep led by a lion than one hundred lions led by a sheep."
– Charles Maurice de Talleyrand-Périgord, French diplomat.

When I think of Donald Trump, I picture the iconic scene in Stanley Kubrick's 1964 classic *Dr. Strangelove or: How I Learned to Stop Worrying and Love the Bomb* – Major "King" Kong straddling an atomic bomb to oblivion.

The image captures the fragility of affairs during the Cold War, when any moment could have led to an atomic showdown and the end of the world. The film satirises "redneck" America's longstanding inclination towards violence in situations of conflict. Like Major Kong, America's new president embodies right-wing rhetoric and hillbilly, trigger-happy sentiment.

"I would bomb the shit out of 'em," Trump famously said of ISIS in the buildup to the US election.

Actually, there are protocols that governments undertake to observe before declaring war on any foreign state. I don't expect a reality TV star who has no training or background in governance to know this. Yet, despite his lack of experience in public office, Trump is the new president of the United States. As surreal as it is, Trump is just one example of a growing global trend: the rise of businessmen in politics.

Europe's debt crisis, China's imploding economy and a global student debt problem are some of the factors driving a new global recession, according to economists all over the world. The divide between rich and impoverished people is deepening daily and many see deteriorating living conditions as a failure of the politicians steering the ship.

Men like Trump, whose public relations teams have molded an image of financial success in trying times, begin to look like the answer to these failures. If they were able to build multi-billion dollar businesses from the ground up, they must know how to resolve the economic challenges facing a country.

Desperate people fed up with struggling through each day might think that men like Trump have the answers, but this thinking is dangerous. There is a reason why blurring the line between business and government is frowned upon.

A business approach to governance does very little for ordinary people; in fact, they become nothing more than a resource in the production line of capital. At worst, politicians who are businessmen can manipulate government policy to benefit their private business ventures. This is not a far-fetched suggestion.

Take Paraguay's current president, Horacio Cartes. Cartes is a businessman who started his political career just under a decade ago. He gained prominence due to his thriving business empire which includes everything from beverage production to owning a soccer club. Cartes has been suspected of involvement in criminal cigarette smuggling, and Paraguay has been slow to implement international legislation aimed to reduce cigarette smoking. The tobacco industry, his cash cow.

In South Africa, many have pinned Deputy President Cyril Ramaphosa as the next presidential candidate for the ruling party. The mining mogul, hailed as one of South Africa's richest men, has demonstrated a disconnect in the way that he dealt with protesting miners in Marikana.

Ramaphosa's calls for "concomitant action" as per his email to Lonmin chief commercial officer Albert Jamieson allegedly led to the massacre which claimed 34 lives. Ramaphosa has since been exonerated by the Marikana Commission report, but his involvement is a far cry from his days as secretary of the National Union of Mineworkers, and demonstrates that business links influence how they lead and interests they prioritise.

Granted, the deputy president has been instrumental in pushing for a national minimum wage at the National Economic Development and Labour Council (NEDLAC), acting as a buffer between Business and Labour. However, negotiations were meant to have been finalised months ago. Such is the course of any pro-people policy: promises, delays, protests, promises…

It is clear that people have grown tired of empty promises. They seek the tenacity of the proverbial lion to protect their interests. But, the risk one hundred sheep take under the leadership of a lion is that lions are carnivorous cats.

THE DAILY VOX (2016)

RAMAPHOSA IS A BUSINESSMAN. SO IS TRUMP. STILL REASSURED?

Chapter 12

"A President I Can Be Proud of': South Africans Express Their Hopes," proclaimed the New York Times upon the announcement of Cyril Ramaphosa as South Africa's new commander-in-chief. The rand recovered overnight from its decade-long slump, and white people started unpacking bags with one hand and canceling one-way flights to Australia with the other.

We had grown so tired of the blatant abuse by one man — a certain Jacob Zuma — that we've found ourselves curled up in bed with another — a wealthy one at that — dreaming of all the wonderful things to come.

White folk took to social media posting their selfies with Ramaphosa on the Sea Point promenade, those outside Cape

Town settled for making him their profile pic — hell, they were ten seconds away from changing their relationship statuses on Facebook. Then, in the month of Valentine, he dropped the "expropriation bomb", breaking their fragile hearts into pieces.

He left them traumatised by his announcement of land expropriation without compensation, because how can a man serving their interests "business interests" side with the enemy?

Simple. It's business, sweetheart. Don't take it personally. And before he leaves all the Black folk reveling in the revolutionary light of Uhuru dumbfounded, I would like to remind everyone that Cyril Ramaphosa is a businessman. And businessmen care about nothing more than the bottom line.

Just last year, I voiced my apprehension about this global trend of electing businessmen into office, citing instances of how these same business people corrupt governance, twisting and bending public policy to advance their business interests. Although universal, my warnings were specifically about Donald Trump... and just look what happened there.

Does anybody remember his early days in office? Trump, distracting the US with a proclamation that he is building a wall to block off Mexico, had the whole country debating the merits and logistics of this wall, while he presidentially signed off on more anti-the-whole-world "executive orders" than any other US president. Some of which would benefit his business friends.

It has been but a few months, and already our dear president is pulling Trump tactics of misdirection and undercover policy pushes on us.

While we're all trying to figure out how to hold on to the land that we own, how to expropriate (without compensation) the land that we'd like to own, and for some, how to stop paying the bank for land that we kind of own, Ramaphosa is trying to sign off on a bill that will allow mining companies easier access to land rich with minerals.

Buried in the 99-page Traditional and Khoi-San Leadership Bill is a clause giving traditional leaders licence to enter into agreements with investors in respect of communal land, without consent from those whose customary land rights stand to be compromised.

In short, it would legitimise unlawful and corrupt sales of communal land to mining companies without consultation or accountability, as far as monies exchanged is concerned.

Yes, Ramaphosa gave up all business interests to fulfill his duties as president, but certain members of his family are still coining it from the mining sector — and needless to say, stand to benefit from the loophole the bill creates.

(Now, I bet everybody's thinking about the part in *Miners Shot Down* when they go over the emails between Ramaphosa and Lonmin's chief commercial officer; you know: where he calls for "concomitant action" against the so-called criminal strikers.)

But honestly, that anyone expects the NUM-leader-turned-McDonalds-multimillionaire to suddenly put the people first is mind-boggling; he literally sold heart attacks with a side of chips.

So before getting too comfortable, picking out new bedding to snuggle up in as the cold of winter sets in, I suggest we remember that our beloved president is a shrewd businessman, ready to kick us out of his bed — without taxi money, even.

HUFFINGTON POST (2018)

STILL IN THE DARK: HIV AND BLACK PEOPLE

Chapter 13

With new infection rates and Aids-related deaths on a decline globally, it seems we are finally gaining ground in the race toward the end of HIV. But, an alarming world trend in new HIV infections suggests that certain people have been left at the wayside: Black people.

In an open letter to the US Centre for Disease Control and Prevention, the LA-based Aids Healthcare Foundation noted that while African-Americans made up a mere 12% of the total US population, they accounted for close to half of new infections in the country. Yet, only one in every ten people on PrEP (a drug which stops you from contracting HIV) were black.

"We call on you to re-balance your prevention efforts to align with what patients want and need so that we can achieve better success in preventing new infections," it signed off.

As an HIV-prevention campaigner, I know very well the struggle of addressing the "wants and needs" of people more likely to get HIV. We are guilty of making broad assumptions about their daily lives – I suppose, a consequence of the shoestring budgets at our disposal.

"Black African men and women are advised to have an HIV test and a regular HIV and STI screen if having unprotected sex with new or casual partners," suggests HIV in UK – Situation Report 2015 for targeted HIV-prevention messaging.

This report found that even in the UK where white people make up the larger population of people living with HIV, Black people were more likely to contract HIV because it was much more prevalent in that minority population.

However, making sweeping assumptions about black sexuality is counterproductive as it feeds social stigma attached to the virus, a major driver of HIV, deterring people from seeking healthcare and family planning because others might talk.

Growing up in what has been dubbed the world's HIV capital, South Africa, I am all too familiar with racist rhetoric blaming high HIV prevalence in Black people on wayward sexual behaviours which are, in fact, false.

The fact of the matter is, as Brazilian researcher Kia Caldwell, points out, HIV is spread due to socio-economic circumstance and not bad sex habits.

In a 2016 report on how HIV affects Afro-Brazilian females, Caldwell stressed the need for an intersectional approach to HIV research and health policy in her home country, which saw a decline in new HIV infections in all population groups but black females.

She blames the Afro-Brazilian experience of HIV on poverty and violence, and a lack of access to healthcare and employment, perpetuated by structural bias based on skin colour.

The South African Studies in Poverty and Inequality Institute noted this exact experience in its 2013 study of access to healthcare in South Africa. It found that while healthcare services are available, poor Black people were less likely to visit local clinics as it often meant a day of unpaid leave.

A researcher friend working in rural South Africa once told me that in addition, many people in these more remote communities are struggling to have sex safely, even if they wanted to. For instance, for a lot of men-who-sleep-with-men in these communities, access to a safe setting for sex is hard to come by, let alone condoms or the time to find them.

The intricacies in the way HIV affects different communities can no longer be ignored if we are to achieve UNAids 90-90-90 goals by 2020. The inclusion of local voices in HIV research, messaging and advocacy is essential – and I am not the only one who thinks so. UNAids states in its 2016 global HIV update:

"Beneath this global figure lie multiple disparities—across regions, within countries, between men and women and young and old, and among specific populations being left behind. These disparities must be addressed in order to achieve the reductions required to end the Aids epidemic as a public health threat by 2030."

If we are to stop the spread of HIV, we need to understand the real reasons why it's still spreading in certain communities. To that end, including the voices of those most at risk is vital.

THE MTV STAYING ALIVE FOUNDATION (2016)

HIV: OUNCE OF PREVENTION IS WORTH A POUND OF CURE

Chapter 14

Despite monumental feats in the fight against HIV in recent years, we are nowhere close to the end of this battle.

For as long as key risk populations are denied access to groundbreaking treatment, any breakthrough is simply null and void; without proper access to relevant treatment and health services, those most vulnerable will continue to bear the brunt of the pandemic.

A quick Google search of "HIV in South Africa" is all it takes to witness the greatest health conundrum we've yet faced – and perhaps the obvious answer to that same predicament. For every headline celebrating new miracle HIV drugs, you will find one pointing out growing infection rates among young girls who sleep with older men, and men who sleep with men (MSM).

This has been the trend for as long as we've made the distinction between HIV and Aids, and that it still continues in this fashion even in light of these "miracle drugs" is a sure indication that our prevention interventions are completely out of sync.

Pre-Exposure Prophylaxis (PrEP), the most recent addition to the mix of HIV-prevention efforts, helps those who stick to the strict treatment regime from contracting HIV.

The wonderful thing about this drug is the autonomy it affords users, particularly young women who often are unable to negotiate condom use with their sex partners for a host of reasons, which is a major contributing factor to high HIV rates within this key population group.

But PrEP is not yet widely accessible in the public sector in South Africa. It is only available through demonstration sites, clinical research institutes and the private sector. A month's supply costs between R300 and R550 from the private sector and not all medical aids will cover the cost.

Apart from a special intervention targeting MSM in certain provinces, PrEP is only given to HIV-negative people who self-identify as being at substantial risk of acquiring HIV.

And if we've learnt anything from HSRC's Stigma Index (2014) it's that people are already petrified about what seeking sexual reproductive health services says about them. So how many young girls do we expect to declare their sexual behaviour as "risky" at the local clinic?

Yet, our government remains confident in its plans to curb the estimated 2,000 HIV infections that occur weekly in South Africa among women between the ages of 15 and 24. However, if one looks at HIV interventions that have been successful in South Africa, it becomes blatantly clear that universal access to treatment is key.

The only reason for the drastic drop in mother-to-child transmission of the virus is because pregnant women in the public healthcare system have no choice but to be screened for HIV – and, if positive, undergo treatment to ensure that their babies are born healthy.

The number of Aids-related deaths have halved over the past decade simply because our government made antiretroviral therapy available to all who need it. But while these successes are outstanding, considering the scale of our HIV problem, an ounce of prevention is still worth a pound of cure, especially from a cost perspective.

New research in the US shows that while antiretroviral therapy has helped people with HIV live longer, their organs tend to age faster. What this means for our public health sector is an increase in cases of illness associated with old age, such as heart disease and diabetes.

Any money saved by skimping on budgets for preventive treatment will eventually be needed for treatment of other illnesses caused by the virus down the line. In trying to be penny wise our government is being rather pound foolish.

With viable preventative measures available, any excuse to prolong this vicious cycle is exactly that: an excuse. Just another way that old men are ruining the lives of young South African girls.

THE SUNDAY TIMES (2018)

BRING BACK OUR GIRLS: REINVENTION. INTERVENTION

Chapter 15

What surprises me most about this entire situation is not the fact that young girls are being used as collateral in an ideological war, but that we've allowed it to get to this point. While the #bringbackourgirls narrative is nothing new to a continent in conflict, stepping back from such instances in an era of advocacy for an African collective in decision-making is counterproductive toward the cause our leaders are trying to sell.

As an International Relations graduate, I am well aware of the restrictions to intervention within a country's borders because of their right to sovereignty. I know that there are all sorts of procedures that need to be followed before any external state or entity is allowed to step into any country's domestic disputes. But, our leaders – the same ones who go around preaching "African Renaissance", upholding the idea of African solutions to Africa's problems – have established through the African Union that intervention may take place if a member country is not able to manage internal conflict. The fact that the West had been called in to intervene is an indication that such a point was reached. The question remains, though: If we had acted sooner, would we have been able to curb the situation?

Sadly, we'll never know; but quite frankly, I'd rather us have tried and failed than sit in the situation we find ourselves in. The possibility of successfully retrieving the kidnapped girls would have been worth the resources utilised. A simple OFFICIAL response – any response at that – would have sent out a message to the world and Africans would need reminding that we are serious about our stance on Gender-Based Violence and the empowerment of the girl child, and not just jumping hoops for brownie points from international funders who have placed the address of gender inequalities at the top of the global agenda.

I understand the idea that good fences make good neighbours, but a white suburban approach to politics is a slap in the face to the notion of Ubuntu – that warm fuzzy feeling that supposedly makes us Africa. What is Ubuntu? Well, it is not just some fluffy notion of community that marketing firms exploit and misrepresent in their media messages. Anyone who's grown up in a previously-Black neighbourhood will tell you that your neighbour's issues are your issues – and when warranted, issues are dealt with as a collective, as a community. It is that blurred line between the "stranger" next door and those living in your home that is Ubuntu. It seems that ever since our top dogs have moved into the leafy suburbs, they've completely forgotten this way of life.

I recently moved into one such suburb and was really alarmed when I requested that the authorities intervene in a violent domestic dispute next door. I was shocked that despite several eyewitnesses to the incident, the police made no arrests because the home owner's wife told them it was just a misunderstanding. Last week, a domestic abuse case in

Ekurhuleni made headlines because police failed to intervene sooner. *Beeld* newspaper reported that a man held his family hostage for years, electrocuting his children and burning them with a blow torch. One neighbour said that she notified the police about this man's heinous activities several times and that they only stepped in when his 11-year-old son managed to escape the house. The mother – who remained silent for all of these years – only cracked regarding the abuse due to police pressure.

President Goodluck Jonathan's initial response to the kidnapped girls was similar to that of these abused women. He even issued a release to the media announcing the return of the girls – which he retracted a few hours later – in a bid to save face, and perhaps political credibility, in an awful situation.

The problem at both a local and continental scale, as I see it, lies in the fact that we (Africans) have not yet molded institutional responses to situations like these – responses that are rooted in our own beliefs and ideology. Most of our laws stem from colonial law enforced by "past" oppressors. While we have identified that legislation of this nature has been designed to disenfranchise African states, the few who have the power to advance this agenda are too comfortable where they reside to realise the plight of ordinary Africans.

Think about it, the only time we really saw an African response to the kidnapping of these girls was after Michelle Obama set the agenda on social media. It saddens me that almost two centuries after slavery was abolished, we are still waiting for the permissions of our slave masters to think, let alone act. What value is there to our freedom when our leaders have not broken free from their shackles? What power do I, as an individual, have to make a change in society when the chains of oppression tightly bind the legislation that is meant to enable me? With this in mind, how are we able to respond to situations like a kidnapping at this scale when we are failing to handle domestic issues at a much smaller scale?

I am optimistic about the aims of the African Union and the idea of an "African Renaissance" – for so long as the powers that be see it as a reality and not just a selling point to investors, tourists and potential voters – and I am of the view that bringing back OUR girls would be a good place to start in the reinvention of the African continent.

LOVELIFE (2014)

THE SCRAMBLE TO DUMP PLASTIC IS 'WASTE COLONIALISM'

When Namibia declared its independence in 1990, it officially marked the end of colonialism on the African continent. But, while most African nations have been free of European rule for a number of decades now, it seems that the power dynamics have only really changed in principle.

In 1960, the United Nations (UN) General Assembly adopted the Declaration on the Granting of Independence to Colonial Countries and Peoples, known also as the Declaration on Decolonization. This resolution solemnly proclaimed the necessity of bringing colonialism in all its forms and manifestations to a speedy and unconditional end.

Herein lies the problem. The assumption that statehood is the be all and end all to decolonisation is short-sighted and stifling to any real progress. Granted, a country's independence is a massive milestone, all considered; however, it simply cannot end there.

The continued exploitative relationship between countries in the global majority and their former colonisers erode the foundation of their liberty. There are many "forms and manifestations" in which colonialism still lingers right here on the African continent.

Be it the fact that 14 African countries continue to pay "colonial tax" to France, or that Spanish fishing vessels see nothing wrong with looting our waters. These old colonial habits are very hard to break; the convenience of the West always seems to take precedence over ours.

Take, for example, the way that countries like the United States (US) scrambled to dump their plastic waste in Africa and other Asian countries after China pulled the plug on their ludicrous arrangement of shipping almost all of its waste there for decades.

A recent Greenpeace report found that after China refused to accept their waste, they simply moved on to the next so-called 'developing nation' they could find. And if *The Guardian's* figures are anything to go by then over 1 billion tons of plastic was dumped in countries like Senegal and Kenya in the single year that followed this development.

And, even after plastic was added to the list of illegal biohazardous waste outlawed by the Basel Convention, American petrochemical lobbyists still tried to undermine Kenya's domestic anti-plastic laws to flood African countries – more specifically the 27 nations signed to the African Free Trade Agreement – with plastic.

As we speak, there are illicit shipments of plastic waste stuck in Liberia and Tunisia, and authorities in each country have exhausted every diplomatic avenue to repatriate the hundreds of containers to their respective countries of origin – Greece and Italy.

These countries have no respect for the laws they collectively come up with and vote into place, let alone the laws of our countries, which serve to benefit our people. They only recognise our sovereignty when it suits them; and when it doesn't, we quickly switch back into wastelands they've tried to turn us into for centuries.

The way that plastic waste is simply shipped off to countries in the global majority is quite colonial in its approach – dare I call it, 'waste colonialism'. Its impact on underprivileged nations is certainly as destructive as the looting and enslavement that categorised the colonial era, because it is breeding environments for people that are practically the same.

The UN Environment Programme released a report this year about how plastic pollution – and by virtue, its production – has a disproportionate impact on poorer communities and countries. It found that these communities experienced high rates of environmental injustice, and that these communities were most likely to comprise people of colour.

The people of colour living in these communities and countries not only experienced the discomfort of superficial environmental degradation due to plastic pollution, but they were also more likely to fall ill from air pollution surrounding the plants they have to migrate to in search of low-paying jobs. And, as research by Studies in Poverty and Inequality Institute has demonstrated, low-wage earners are not likely to miss work and seek medical attention in fear of job loss.

If we are still made to bear the brunt for the sake of Western countries' comfort, just how different is that from the status quo under colonial rule? What good has this so-called freedom done for those of us that are not part of the political elite, apart from claiming new national identities?

A rose by any other name would smell as sweet, no? The same can be said for colonialism in its current manifestation. Its stench is unbearable, but conveniently shipped to our countries to deal with.

DAILY MAVERICK (2021)

CLASSIFICATION OF KHOI-SAN AS COLOURED STUNTS SOCIETY'S ABILITY TO IMAGINE THEM AS ANYTHING BUT

Chapter 17

"**H**istory is a people's memory, and without a memory, man is demoted to the lower animals. When you have no knowledge of your history, you're just another animal."

– Malcolm X, 1964.

A recent Human Rights Commission (HRC) report noted the importance of officially recognising the cultural identity of Khoi and San peoples on an equal standing to other cultural groups as "inextricably" linked to human dignity.

It identified the continued forced apartheid classification of Khoi-San peoples as "Coloured" as an infringement on their right to identity and culture, a precursor to "their virtual political and social invisibility".

The commission, as mandated by the SAHRC Act, recommended that the South African government, through the Presidency and Department of Arts and Culture, begin taking steps toward the removal of this forced categorisation by 31 March 2019.

These findings add a new dimension to public discourse around the authenticity of those categorised as Coloured and their African identity. Its contribution to what has been deemed "the Coloured debate" is simple: the Khoi-San cannot rebuild identity and social structures in the absence of recognition.

Continued exclusion only stands to push them further into the margins of society as inadequate measures to promote, protect and preserve their culture, traditions and traditional knowledge systems will lead to the complete erasure of their heritage: their memory.

As it stands, our constitution only recognises the Khoi-San under language provisions in Section 6. Any reference to "indigenous" in other provisions is interpreted and understood to mean all African communities.

Associate Professor at the Centre for Humanities Research at the University of Western Cape, Suren Pillay, credits this disqualification of indigenous status to race categorisation.

"Across the continent there were often categories of populations who did not fit neatly into (the) division of white settler and black native," he writes.

"They were often categories of populations defined as ethnic, but like the Europeans, they were classified as races under colonial law. Like Europeans, colonial thinking said they came from elsewhere, and were also therefore not indigenous."

This has manifested in an unfairly stringent process in order for Khoi-San to prove their identity. While other African tribes are granted recognition based on language, surname or customary practices, the recently passed Traditional and Khoi-San Leadership Bill prescribes strict criteria for a community to be recognised as Khoi-San.

The bill affirms that to gain recognition as such, a community must have a history of self-identification and must be separate from all other communities; they must observe distinctive established Khoi-San customary laws and customs; and must have a track record of existence within a specific geographical area.

On top of this, Khoi-San leaders are required to submit membership lists to the government on an annual basis – comprising full names and surnames of members, with certified copies of the identity documents.

Time and again, Khoi-San leadership, particularly in the Northern and Western Cape, has lodged its grievances about this type of unfair treatment.

In the most recent attempt to capture the attention of the government and the South African public at large, Khoi-San King Calvin Cornelius III served notice to Parliament to vacate its Cape Town premises.

The eviction notice given to Cabinet, and addressed to the president, read:

"This is to officially inform you of the decision of the King and the Khoi-San people to secede from South Africa. You were given notice of our secession as well as our declaration based on the principle of self-determination and independence to establish the Sovereign State of Good Hope."

It set an impossible five-day notice period, accompanied by a 48-hour registration allowance for non-Khoi-San "aliens" to legally reside in the independent Khoi-San state; it pretty much mirrors the hoops Khoi-San peoples are expected to jump through to validate their existence.

The forced classification of Khoi-San as Coloured stunts society's ability to imagine them as anything but. It legally permits the denial and erasure of their existence, unique history and memory. Thus, not only does it strip them of their identity, but their humanity too.

DAILY MAVERICK (2018)

JOEY RASDIEN: BLASPHEMY, BIGOTRY AND THE OTHER B-WORD

Chapter 18

"It doesn't matter what @joeyrasdien said, racist comments from Indian Muslims like 'Boesman never went to madressa' are unacceptable."

– Shaeera Kalla tweeted on July 23.

Racist insults hurled at comedian Joey Rasdien after his recent controversial performance took me back to a time shortly after our first democratic election, when I was but one of two Coloured learners attending a predominantly Indian school.

I didn't look like other children (despite being half Indian) and while I noticed this difference, I never quite understood just how different I was to the other kids until, one day, my Coloured counterpart told me that we needed to stand together because we were "the only *ones* in the school".

It suddenly made sense to me why I had so few friends; it made sense why I was always the last to be chosen on a side when we played or why I was never invited over to hangout on the weekend. Also, it made sense why Indian teachers never bothered pushing me academically the way they did their own kind; and why *I* was always the one in trouble with teachers, even if we were all doing the same exact thing. All the time I had imagined that it was because I was Christian, but other (Indian) Christians in my class were more readily accepted into cliques.

I must have been eight at the time; what did I know about standing together because we were "the only *ones* in school"? As time progressed and we became more and more aware of our differences, standing together became more and more important. After-lunch break arguments quickly polarised classrooms by ethnicity, religion, race. Without intervention by teachers, principals or any other adult, things easily escalated into racist, bigoted screaming matches – and sometimes, these would cross the generational line into teacher-pupil disputes.

I always joked that I have been called bushman so many times in my youth that it literally turned my caramel skin thick; but the reality is, and though people seldom resort to that type of racism anymore, it makes my heart sink every single time I hear it.

I know a lot of people identify as *boesman*, and some of my family and friends claim the term *bushy* as a term of endearment or belonging; but, my personal experience with the word has only ever been derogatory and it makes me uncomfortable, to say the least. Let's face it, when used outside of our own community, it almost always serves to degrade us.

That people feel confident enough to racially attack Rasdien publicly speaks volumes about perceptions of Coloured South Africans; as if our marginalisation begs the way to such degradation without consequence.

People are very careful about using the k-word when it comes to South Africa's Bantu population because, as in the case of the infamous Penny Sparrow, there will be hell to pay: R200,000 fines, job loss, criminal records... This is not because she insulted a particular group of people, but because that particular group of people mobilised, tracked her down and sought recourse for her assault on their right to dignity.

That is not to say that we have not been proactive enough in protecting our community from insult; the South African Human Rights Commission recently handled a case in Limpopo where the complainant claimed he was repeatedly called a "*fokken boesman*" and told to "go back to Cape Town" by South African Police Services officials. I am, however, saying that perhaps we are not doing enough to demonstrate the muscle of our resilient community.

My childhood friend was onto something all those years ago when he told me it was important to stand together as "the only *ones* in school"; evidently, not too much has changed since then. The toils of Coloured South Africans remain a crass joke, one we can no longer tolerate.

THE DAILY VOX (2017)

THE WORD 'BOESMAN' FALLS INTO THE SAME CATEGORY AS THE K-WORD AND MUST BE OUTLAWED

Chapter 19

The recent racist rant by the ANC mayor of Welkom demonstrates the literal danger of allowing apartheid-era slurs like 'boesman' to be used in post-democratic South Africa.

In a video that circulated on social media recently, Welkom Mayor Nkosinjani Speelman used the term *"boesman"* to describe Coloured people during an address to members of the South African National Defence Force ahead of their deployment into communities during the countrywide Covid-19 lockdown.

Speelman also played on apartheid stereotypes of the Coloured community, calling them unruly drunkards, as he encouraged soldiers not to hesitate to *"skop en donner"* (kick and beat) the people of Bronville. There was an outcry from members of the public, especially Coloured people. The SA Human Rights Commissioner in the Free State, Thabang Kheswa, confirmed the receipt of several complaints over Speelman's comments.

ANC officials decided to temporarily suspend the Welkom mayor, both a member of the party and a public representative, for violating the provision in its constitution that prohibits all forms of racist utterances. He has since made a public apology in which he justified his racism as a "slip of the tongue".

"It was not undermining you – it was just out of mistake. So, I want to apologise to everybody from Bronville, in particular the Coloured people," Speelman said. "I was not saying it in a bad spirit; it was just a slip of the tongue – to say that these people are giving us a problem … I am humble, I feel so sorry for what I have said."

The South African Human Rights Commission (SAHRC) however, was not satisfied with the apology. In a media statement, the commission said it viewed his utterances in a very serious light and that Speelman's apology would not suffice. They committed to a full investigation after the current Covid-19 lockdown – which would also look into other allegations of human rights violations by the city in its failure to serve the community.

This is not the first time that the Coloured community has pursued legal action against the use of the word, which has long been used to dehumanise them in southern Africa. But this particular incident may just lead to the necessary restrictions of its use under our democratic dispensation.

In 2008, Jacobus Faasen submitted to the Equality Court that, as a descendant of the KhoiSan, he found the use of the word *"boesman"* by *Die Burger* newspaper to be hate speech because it disregarded his human dignity. He argued that it was derived from the word *"bosjesman"*, which meant baboon, or orangutan.

The court did not rule in Faasen's favour, however, they found that the newspaper's usage was not malicious. And in the years that followed, several cases of this nature have been brought before a variety of tribunals, all with the same outcome, based on the same principle: Intent.

During the 2013 strike at Glencore Xstrata in Sekhukhune, the *Mail & Guardian* reported that an employee complained of being called a *"boesman"* by a white employee. In a report, the presiding officer ruled that the slur was an accepted nickname of the employee.

SABC1's *Khumbul'ekhaya* came under fire in 2016 when Frederick Smith complained to the Broadcasting Complaints Commission of South Africa that an episode of the show was offensive when it referred to Coloured people in a "manner that is racist, insulting and defamatory".

In the episode, a Xitsonga-speaking individual referred to a Coloured person as a *"boesman"*. The television network translated the word to "Coloured person" in its English subtitles to clarify what she meant. The complaint was dismissed. The commission stated that the word was not intended to be used in a demeaning way.

The precedent set by the 2008 Equality Court ruling allowed for the continued use of the term, despite numerous expressions of its negative impact on the dignity of the Coloured community. For as long as it was not meant with ill intention, it was fine under the law. And as demonstrated in Speelman's case, this remains the go-to justification for those called out for its usage.

When Penny Sparrow called Black beachgoers "monkeys" in a 2016 Facebook post, she was slapped with a R150,000 fine – despite arguing that her intent was not racist because she found primates to be cute, but messy. Her *crimen injuria* conviction shifted the way our courts deal with incidents of racism, coming down harder on convicted racists, sending a clear message of intolerance of hate speech.

The most recent example of this was that of Adam Catzavelos, who was also fined R150,000 and made to publicly apologise for his use of the k-word in a 22-second online video. In another case, estate agent Vicky Momberg was sentenced to three years in prison after throwing a racist temper tantrum, where she used the slur several times against Black law enforcement officers.

The use of the k-word is so severely restricted in our country because it was acknowledged by the Constitutional Court in *SARS v CCMA (2017 (1) SA 549 (CC)* to be "the worst insult that can ever be visited upon an African person in South Africa". There are no gray areas; it is not to be used to describe another person, by law.

The "b-word" carries that same weight in the Coloured community, and should hold the same restrictions on its usage regardless of so-called intent, or its adoption into vernacular languages under apartheid rule – after all, we have evidently made great progress in phasing out this type of language.

Speelman's SAHRC investigation will quite likely find him guilty of hate speech. Unlike the incidents before, there is no confusion about his intent – not only had he advocated hatred toward Coloured people by stereotyping them, he attempted to incite violence against this community. He should be held to the same level of account as those in recent years.

The Welkom mayor has clearly demonstrated the danger of providing allowance for the usage of apartheid-era slurs. These words are not only loaded for those on the receiving end, but they are also laced with hatred harboured during our painful past. In the wrong hands, they can quite literally be a loaded gun.

DAILY MAVERICK (2020)

#COLOUREDEXCELLENCE: WHY DOES EVERYTHING HAVE TO BE ABOUT RACE?

Chapter 20

"The most potent weapon of the oppressor is the mind of the oppressed."

– Steve Biko, 1978.

As quickly as Wayde van Niekerk shattered the 17-year-old 400m world record at the Rio Olympics, social networks were abuzz with news of the South African sprinter's victory – but as the world celebrated his remarkable feat, the community of his origin was slated for claiming the victory as its own.

Debate flared on for hours following his race, with everyone from academics to rap artists weighing in. Its result: a long overdue hashtag #ColouredExcellence, and perhaps the answer to the age-old question "Why must everything be about race?" posed as the main charge against South Africa's proud Coloured community.

Racial tension around the world has forced media workers to begin questioning their role in reinforcing social perceptions which are harmful and negative.

Global leadership nonprofit organisation, The Aspen Institute, noted during a 2014 roundtable on community change with a group of very influential journalists in Washington DC: "The chief mandate of good journalism is to inform and educate, and journalists play a vital role in shaping perceptions about social groups."

The institute added that contextualising news events through an analysis of data and history could potentially achieve an understanding of the complexities of race needed to illuminate the roots of long-running racial disparities.

I've noticed this in South African media where, ever since the notion of the "Black diamond" emerged a decade ago, Black professionals grace the cover of magazines and business sections of newspapers which celebrate their success in the face of gross adversity. This has made a huge impact on the psyche of the Black community, particularly the youth, because these are people who grew up like them, and have made it.

The Coloured community is not afforded the same media presence because, quite frankly, they can't match the spending power of the 80% Black majority population – and the only time they capture the media is when they disrupt the motions of those with spending power: crime, service delivery protests and, apparently, threats to national security.

The result of this lack of interest in the Coloured community is that the violent, volatile and illiterate South African Coloured narrative has not evolved beyond these apartheid stereotypes developed to disenfranchise the community. Deliberate or not, the reinforcement of these stereotypes in the media says to this community – and others – it's all Coloureds will ever be.

This Heritage Month sees the nationwide release of the movie *Noem My Skollie*, which boasts the largest ensemble of Coloured actors in cinema history. It tells the story of four Coloured adolescents from the Cape Flats forced into gangsterism, two of whom are later arrested and become legendary storytellers in Pollsmoor Prison.

This movie is based on a fascinating true story and is a huge deal for the community; except, the last major Coloured-focused cinematic release, *Four Corners*, also dealt with gangsterism and jail.

The South African Institute of Race Relations released a report in 2008 stating that while Black people accounted for the greater number of the prison population, the imprisonment rate of Coloured people was twice that of their black counterparts. The numbers have hardly changed since then.

Some may argue that these are the realities of the community being depicted, but how do you expect to inspire change in a community when all you focus on is what damages them?

Human beings are rational creatures and you would expect them to critically engage with messages being presented to them by media. But as the so-called fourth estate, the media is pretty much positioned as a reliable, authoritative source of information which decreases resistance to what they present.

As Malcolm X noted in 1963: "The media's the most powerful entity on earth. They have the power to make the innocent guilty and to make the guilty innocent, and that's power. Because they control the minds of the masses."

This is why van Niekerk's victory is crucial to the Coloured community, because someone who once struggled to gain the recognition due to him just over a year ago (possibly because of the racial politics in media described above) cannot be ignored right now, is larger than life, and Coloured!

A mere 43.3 seconds was all it took for the Kraaifontein native to shatter the bonds of what we know as Coloured: #ColouredExcellence. He represents something so much bigger; the Coloured you never knew existed... and the community can begin to redefine its heritage and continue to do so, as change is constant.

As former Minister of Finance, Trevor Manuel, once said: "This generation, our generation of people who benefited, must always be the pioneers who look to younger people and say mediocrity is not accommodated in what we do."

THE DAILY VOX (2016)

DID THE COLOURED COMMUNITY WIN IDOLS SA THIS YEAR?

Chapter 21

So, a Coloured girl from Bishop Lavis won Idols on Sunday night, and some people on Twitter are mad because they believe that Coloured people stayed up late all week, finishing their airtime voting for her.

I refuse to believe that Paxton Fielies' win was based solely on the so-called Coloured vote. This 17-year-old transitioned between screaming "Oh my God!" and hitting notes perfectly, with the greatest of ease, during the show's finale. She is undeniably extremely talented.

As Idols SA judge Unathi Msengana noted a couple of weeks ago, Paxton performs to her target audience: the youth demographic, who are constantly on their phones with loads of disposable cash (if they have DSTV in their homes, they almost certainly have pocket money to spare). She is marketing gold.

Having said that, I'd like to explore the notion that Coloured people mobilise and vote for contestants on talent shows; firstly, because this always seems to be the response to Coloured contestants winning talent shows on TV; and secondly, because, yes, it is certainly a contributing factor to her victory.

Along with a host of anti-Coloured rhetoric that followed the show were pockets of jubilant displays by Coloured Twitter users, proud to see one of their own taking the highly contested prize – a mini resurgence of the #ColouredExcellence buzz that followed Wayde van Niekerk's record-breaking win at the Rio Olympics.

For them, Paxton represents a girl from the Cape Flats who managed to defy all odds and become a household name, with a lucrative record deal behind her. She represents the hopes and dreams of the majority of Coloured people who remain stuck in absolute destitution. As trivial as reality shows are, her victory is important because it demonstrates that it is possible to exceed society's expectations of you.

Paxton is the beacon of hope for the Coloured community that we don't often see on national television. I have often argued how broadcast media tends to cling onto apartheid stereotypes of the Coloured community out of laziness and lack of representation in the industry – as well as how this does nothing for society's imagination of the Coloured identity.

But, here is a talented Coloured teenager brave enough to stand up in front of millions of people across the country to achieve what she believes in, and in doing so, has the potential to inspire other Coloured youth to prioritise their dreams and to challenge preconceived notions society holds of them.

Paxton is the type of role model the community hardly gets to see in mainstream media, so it shouldn't come as a surprise that Coloured people stood so firmly behind her throughout the course of this season. The community needs these recording-breaking athletes, journalists and superstars to counter images of gangsters, druggies and alcoholics they are so commonly portrayed as – not just to change the way society thinks but that way they think of themselves.

We need to see more representations of Coloured doctors and lawyers, entrepreneurs and innovators if we are ever going to see the first Coloured astronaut, for instance. While it may not be the responsibility of the media to play cheerleader to any faction of society, it is certainly the media's responsibility to dispel ill-conceived notions of communities for the purpose of social cohesion.

However, until such a time that there is a willingness in the media to shift its agenda as far as the Coloured identity is concerned, all this community has in order to achieve such change is its vote. Perhaps, someday, network executives will take this vote (a share of 30 million votes) a lot more seriously.

THE DAILY VOX (2017)

#JUSTICEFORNATHANIELJULIES AND OTHER COLOURED BOYS WITH TARGETS ON THEIR BACKS

Chapter 22

Police gunned a 16-year-old Eldorado Park boy living with Down Syndrome with nothing but biscuits in his hand, allegedly because he couldn't answer them as they interrogated him. Residents say that the officer then dragged him by the neck into the back of a police van, preventing his father from accompanying them to the hospital. When there, police told doctors that he was involved in gang violence.

He died... And when his father finally found his lifeless body at the hospital, he noticed several wounds on Nathaniel Julies' head and chest.

This is certainly not the first time that apartheid stereotypes have been used to justify transgressions against Coloured men. In fact, in our recent history, the Mayor of Welkom Nkosinjani Speelman instructed members of the South African National Defense Force to brutalise members of a Coloured community (whom he referred to using the apartheid slur "boesman") because of how unruly he believed Coloured people behaved under the influence of alcohol.

The shackles of apartheid stereotyping have not only kept us under constant scrutiny, but have allowed many perpetrators to carry out racist agendas against us without fear of retribution. Not surprisingly, Speelman's suspension as a party official was recently cut short, and the South African Human Rights Commission has conveniently forgotten its promise to lodge an investigation into his hate speech as soon as lockdown regulations allowed.

This free-for-all is nowhere more apparent than in our country's incarceration rates, where Coloured males experience imprisonment at a rate twice as high as any other race group. No one ever stopped to ask why that is, because society's perception is that Coloured men are criminals - deviant, at the very least - and so naturally, would end up in jail more frequently.

But has anyone ever considered that perhaps this happens because of what people have been taught to believe about Coloured men? That maybe our people are over-policed out of an irrational fear instilled in the rest of society to keep us in our place.

These divide-and-rule tactics of apartheid maintained the social order of the repressive regime, and justified some of the worst atrocities known to man. It's a legacy we cannot seem to escape; and rears its ugly head every time an irrational act is perpetuated against someone because they just happened to fit the bill.

The police officer(s) in question certainly employed this logic when dealing with Nathaniel Julius; their assumptions about who he must be as a Coloured youth blinded them from the fact that he was disabled - not disruptive, or uncooperative to their questioning. Their predisposition to the members of that community prevented them from recognising his needs, and responding to his vulnerability as a person living with a disability. Racial profiling has led many down this path.

It is a target Jan van Riebeeck placed on our backs when we retaliated against Dutch invasion of the Cape; when they declared our ancestors vermin and then proceeded to systematically hunt them down. It is a target that has remained there for close to four centuries, through one of the most racist regimes the world has ever seen, and is evidently present within the context of our newfound democracy.

How many Coloured men have lost their lives at the hands of the authorities by virtue of their skin? How many have been wrongfully killed, detained and convicted because of this perception that Coloured men are seemingly troublesome?

Every single man entered into our prison system is stripped of any real future and demoted to a subhuman status - turned into the vermin van Riebeeck tried to exterminate. They keep taking our lives, whether we maintain a pulse or not... and I'm not entirely sure that they understand why, themselves.

Nathaniel Julies is just another casualty of a systemic issue rooted in this colonial agenda; an erasure of a people, standing their ground against those draining the resources of this bountiful land. And true to that agenda, the real criminals continue to steal and loot in plain sight; because when everyone stays focused on the so-called threat, who is watching them?

If we are to break the cycle and shake the 400-year-old target off our backs, we need justice to prevail. The police who murdered this Eldorado Park teenager must be brought to book. We need to set a precedent that will discourage others from committing similar transgressions, and make clear that rule of law applies to everybody. Because, if we are not able to hold those abusing power accountable at a grassroots level, what hope is there for accountability all the way at the top?

BRUIN-OU (2020)

A BRUTAL TIME WHEN POLICE WERE HEROES

Chapter 23

I've always known my grandfather to be a hero, long before I knew who he really was to the community.

My cousins all attended school in Bosmont, and would always tell me how their teachers would threaten to call Sgt Louw (as he was affectionately known) whenever their classes got unruly. It always astounded me how much respect everyone around had for him, and that he seemed to be just as much a pillar to an entire community as he was to our family.

My grandfather was always the first to show up in times of despair. He effortlessly juggled being a father and grandfather to his seven living children, their spouses and their children; while instilling in each of us values of responsibility, hope and most importantly, empathy.

But, it was only upon his death that I learned his true contribution to what was once known as Western Coloured Township (Westbury) and its surrounding neighbourhoods. While sorting out his belongings after we laid him to rest, we

"

discovered a treasure trove, a collection of newspaper clippings documenting his relentless crusade on gangsterism which plagued the community in the 1970s - with the help of fearless primary school teacher, Sgt Edwin Augustus.

These articles spoke of how he single-handedly marched 16 gang members into the Newlands Police Station (Sophiatown Police Station) and slept with a pistol under his pillow while admitted at Coronationville Hospital for a week. It was the stuff movies were made of: the lone ranger who risked it all to restore dignity and order to a community torn by violence and terror, one in which school girls carried pangas up their skirts for protection.

It was a joy to read about how the community entrusted him and Sgt Augustus to protect them. It was a far cry from what one reads about the police in the papers these days, with the surge of police brutality around the world. I suppose the difference is that both Augustus and my grandfather were actually from the community they served, and joined the police to make a difference. His commitment to the community's safety led him to establish the country's first shooting club for Black people.

His selfless mission inspired me to continue working toward the empowerment of this community, and communities like this, as writer and activist. His lifelong commitment to this community proved to me that heroes didn't always wear capes and masks - everyday heroes were brave men in plain sight, doing what they could to make a difference.

Heroes were our fathers, our neighbours and our friends. May they forever remain in our memory to inspire hope and evoke change; because the work my grandfather started almost a half century ago is nowhere near complete.

BRUIN-OU (2021)

ADVICE FROM A WRITER WHO HATED READING

Chapter 24

Fifteen years ago, when I was knee deep in adolescence, there stood a big open veld where our local mall is now. The closest mall to Lenasia would take 20 minutes to drive to, or two taxis for those of us commuting via public transport. We didn't have a mall, let alone a conference centre for book fairs where industry leaders could come and share insight on how they broke into industries outside of the norm for township dwellers.

I shared this anecdote with audiences at a book fair I recently spoke at back home, where I sat on a panel trying to figure out why boys (/youth) don't read. My argument: townships do little for the imagination of a young person.

With no writers or journalists in my immediate neighbourhood to get advice from about a career in the media, the future I saw for myself seemed far too risky for my family and community, who'd have rather had me give my CV to the person down the road to get me in at a bank or a call centre.

We have an ugly habit of dampening down on the dreams of township youth, limiting the scope of their futures to customer service and administration – because it's all that we know, because it is "safe".

When you're told you're not going to be able to make it because people like us just don't do *that*, your dreams seem hopeless, so what's the point in making any sort of investment in your future when you're destined (/restricted) to a life much smaller than you imagined for yourself. Why bother picking up a book at all when all you really need to do is scrape through matric?

I never saw the value in reading in my youth – even though I aspired to be a writer, of all things. It always seemed a tedious task; hours and hours could go by, getting through one chapter, weeks to get through a book. If you considered the time it took for me to read a story, you'd understand why it was an investment of my time that I'd never willingly make.

I read set works at school – half-way, anyways – and forced myself through assignment readings at university, never touching the extra articles lecturers included for students interested in learning more. It didn't make sense to me to put in extra work to achieve the same outcome.

My love affair with reading (yes, love affair) began much later in life. One of my mentors, veteran political analyst Nalini Naidoo once said to me that I have strong opinions and I was right about most things I wrote about, but if I really wanted to strengthen my arguments, I would have to back them up with solid facts, adding that no one could dispute factual evidence.

I took her advice, and have been published all over the world because of it. I read as often as I can, and even own an Exclusive

Books reward card now, because the more I know and the more up-to-date I am with developments in my sector, the better my writing (/product) is.

I found a reason to read. I found why it was actually worth my time – and money. In getting young people to read, we need to show them the value of knowledge beyond superficial mantras like "knowledge is power" and truly demonstrate the practicality of reading. Show them how reading can help them achieve their dreams and expose them to a variety of reading options – because the same insight in leather-bound books can easily be found on blogs, with much simpler language too.

Instead of positioning reading as this thing you do in your spare time as a hobby; we need to make it an integral part of their personal development.

That is not to say that we should sell them dreams, we should only encourage theirs; however, education rates do have a direct correlation with employability. A 2015 report by Studies in Poverty and Inequality Institute on the right to basic education in South Africa shows that persons with higher educational attainment are a lot less likely to face unemployment. (... See what I did there?)

If someone wants to become a rapper, encourage them to read biographies, make them realise the importance of understanding business and contracts – how many rappers end up broke because they think they *made it* after being signed? If someone wants to go into beauty, ask them if they read blogs to keep up with trends and techniques, ask them if they know how PH balance affects the way makeup looks on different skin types. If someone has an interest in car modification, make that the entry point to their reading career – who knows, they may just become the only SA importer of some exclusive wheel brand.

We will never win with a 'take a donkey to the well' approach, as the proverb goes, "you cannot force it to drink." A donkey drinks when it is thirsty. If we are ever going to get young people reading, we need to inspire their thirst for it.

LEAD SA (2018)

BUNNY CHOWS AND GUPTAS: THE HERITAGE OF SOUTH AFRICAN INDIANS

Chapter 25

The bunny chow: a dish ingrained in the fabric of South African culture. So much so that its successor, the kota, has been credited as one of the leading causes of obesity in school children.

It owes its origins to the Indian indentured labourers who arrived here in the late 19th Century to be put to work on sugar plantations. Long before Tupperware, their wives would pack leftovers in hollow loaves of bread for them to carry to the fields.

Bunny chow's origin story is one of resilience and ingenuity. It demonstrates how previously disadvantaged people have had to make due in substandard living conditions. One would never guess the loaded cultural significance of the dish while pigging out at the local corner takeaway.

Now, imagine my surprise when a reputable and popular Sunday paper decided the dish deserved a full-page spread to celebrate its heritage, without even making mention of its Indian roots! A township staple, I think they called it, practically positioning as the glue that held *kasi* culture together.

I shouldn't be shocked, really. Contemporary South Africa has made a habit of writing Indian people out of our cultural narrative; you would swear that the Indian diaspora has made absolutely no positive contribution to our heritage or to the development of our nation.

It is as if they just arrived off a boat at Durban Harbour.

Popular "Go back to India" chanting at political rallies or in social media posts is evidence of that. A consequence, I believe, of media coverage of former president Jacob Zuma's illicit relationship with a particular Indian family who almost recolonised the country.

I am not saying that the media shouldn't do its job – thank God it did its job, actually – but what is left is an image of Indian people as corrupt, self-serving and destructive to the masses. All people see now are mini Guptas waiting to steal and rob and control.

Every Indian is suddenly classed in the same category as the (presumed) illegal Somali immigrant opening a shop on the corner, selling (presumed) backdoor goods at prices cheaper than Checkers. Every Indian is assumed to have arrived with the Guptas.

The truth of the matter is that Indians have been around – a lot longer than the 150-year period always cited.

Indians were of the first slaves to arrive in the Cape, but

their slave heritage is always overshadowed by the indentured labourer narrative, which will have you believe that their arrival in South Africa was by choice.

You almost never hear about this, not even when you visit the Imbizo Slave Lodge in Cape Town. In fact, this account of their history is practically limited to a single webpage on *SA History Online.*

This type of omission is mirrored throughout South African history, where Indians were often positioned as allies in the anti-apartheid struggle, but never champions. It is as though they had nothing to struggle against.

We never hear about their subhuman categorisation under past oppressive regimes and the brutality they faced. There are no accounts of how they were often referred to as "*kaffirs met hare* [with hair]" or the other k-word that still finds its way into public dialogue because "that's just what they are called in African languages".

We're definitely not having conversations around reparations – the types of conversations that other slave populations around the world are having, most notably in the West Indies. Economists are not bothered to work out how much Indians have contributed to South Africa's economic growth, or the compound impact of their labour.

It is easy to buy into the Gupta narrative because it is almost the only point of reference that exists for public consumption. It is very difficult to imagine their place in society, and just how deeply their roots run, because of how much we do not know.

THE DAILY VOX (2018)

I WILL NEVER GO BACK TO MY INDIAN BARBER

Chapter 26

As of today, I will never go back to my Indian barber. I once loved going to this barber and I would always suggest him to my friends; but, I have moved on from a place he insists on taking me back to every time I sit in his chair: a place where standards of neatness and beauty were shaped largely by European hair textures and aspirations.

Raju was the type of barber who cut your hair into a style without you having to use tons of product to get it to sit a certain way. Naturally, I was a regular; I sat in his chair fortnightly; he would insist on personally cutting my hair even if any of his employees were free to see me. I always came with new hairstyle ideas and he was always up for the challenge. I really appreciated his attention to detail and that I could call him after hours if I needed a quick trim.

Then came the era of the man bun. While I stopped getting my haircut on account of my topknot, I continued going to him for shaves. During this period, my six-year-old nephew said something really negative about our hair texture; something to effect of "...our hair isn't nice, only spikes are nice", and I made the decision then and there that I would only ever wear my hair in its natural texture because I did not want my nieces and nephews to feel like they didn't have beautiful hair.

My community already has a complex relating to hair texture, a legacy of our apartheid history. Back then, persons of mixed ancestry were classified Coloured, and societal privilege for this particular faction of society was strongly linked to assimilation to whiteness. The apartheid government would literally stick a pencil in your hair to see if it slides out as a determinant of your racial classification.

So, I donned an afro for a few years; it kind of became my signature look; I was 'that guy that looked like Joey Rasdien'. It was amazing to me how much better I looked in my natural hair, how much it reflected my own personality and how it just interrupted the sort of ideas society had about what a young professional looked like. Some of my friends and family didn't like it – my grandmother once said it looked "wild" – but I didn't care and my hair in itself was the implicit middle finger that I never had to show to any of its critics. I have since experimented with other styles.

I was spoiled over the past year – living in the United States – where I would peruse the internet for hair trends for my hair texture, take it to any barbershop and leave an hour later looking like he photocopied it to my scalp. Sure, the average price of a haircut abroad is literally four times the price you'd pay in South Africa, however, I don't believe that my barber back home got it wrong today based on the price.

Being an Indian barber with a largely Indian clientele, perhaps my wavy hair poses a bit of a challenge to Raju, having very little experience with this texture. (Remember, when he cut my hair before in hairstyles for straight hair, he always nailed it.) Fair. I would have probably understood this if he at least attempted to style my hair according to the picture supplied, but, the fade was too high, sides too short and my Mohawk combed in the polar opposite direction to the picture – let's not even talk about texture yet.

It's not that I didn't say anything; I told him he was going too high with the fade, he acknowledged what I said, shook his head and proceeded anyway. I literally had to shout out before he chopped of my short locks which took two months to grow, but by the end of the haircut, he made sure to chop-chop from behind as if I wouldn't notice – at that point, however, I was just like: how much more damage could it have done?

I have noticed this before during a cut and/or shave; always having to remind him to stop cutting. But, I have always dismissed his tendency to cut off more than I would have liked as him trying to earn his money's worth, spending so much time trimming the edges of my beard that I almost have nothing left by the time he's done. However, it struck me today that my barber actually has a disposition to my curls. It's like, to him, my hair is just not styled until he cuts off my curls or combs them out with styling gel. He doesn't seem to want to shave bald all the other Indians who come to him with long hair that stays left when he brushes it to the left.

His bias toward straight hair could stem from the fact that is surrounded by it, or because his understanding of neat hair is part of his conditioning growing up in postcolonial India (since not all Indians have straight hair) or perhaps he feels my hair type is just too stubborn for him; however, I am especially offended by it this time because I specifically asked for my hair to be styled differently. I came with a picture, even. How he didn't see that he was completely off track is beyond me.

My hair will grow back. It will take a little time. Soon enough, I can continue on my crusade on Western – and evidently, Eastern – ideas of what neat hair looks like. I will find a new barber who understands my hair type, who keeps up-to-date with hairstyle trends that suit our people. But, most importantly, I will never ever go back to my Indian barber.

BRUIN-OU (2019)

UN-MAKING A CONTENTED SLAVE

Chapter 27

"I have observed this in my experience of slavery,—that whenever my condition was improved, instead of its increasing my contentment, it only increased my desire to be free, and set me to thinking of plans to gain my freedom."
– Frederick Douglass,
Narrative of the Life of Frederick Douglass.

The National Museum of African-American History and Culture is truly marvelous; eight floors of artifacts and cutting-edge displays honoring Black heritage in this country. The history section tells the story of Black people in a linear fashion, from slavery to Jim Crow, Civil Rights protests and, then, culminates in the election of America's first Black president.

Depending on who you speak to, Obama's presidency was either a major victory for African-American people or a major failure; but, one thing is certain: the former president's term in office unearthed a plethora of truths about the dire socio-economic standing of African-Americans in the United States, that no single executive order could repair.

Many questioned why living conditions for Black people barely improved under the leadership of a Black president whose campaign slogan "Yes, We Can" rang as a promise of it—and many took it upon themselves to answer this question.

A mountain of research emerged demonstrating the nuances of inequality between Black and white Americans: black students carry twice the level of student loan debt, Blacks experience higher default rates on their loans, and to close the wealth gap between Black and white people, the average Black household would have to save 100 percent of its income for three consecutive years.

Ohio State law professor Michelle Alexander detailed how prisons have become the latest form of economic and social disenfranchisement for Black men in *The New Jim Crow: Mass Incarceration in the Age of Colorblindness*. As did Ava DuVernay's documentary *13th*, which explained how a racially-biased legal system literally condemned Black youth to modern-day slavery: stripping them of civic rights and forcing them into slave labour.

It also explored how private companies cashed in on the prison-industrial complex. However, prison businesses are not the only ones cashing in on disparities faced by African-Americans—in fact, corporate American seems adamant on keeping Black people on the slave block.

"I have found that, to make a contented slave, it is necessary to make a thoughtless one. It is necessary to darken his moral and mental vision, and, as far as possible, to annihilate the power of reason."

– Frederick Douglass, continued.

Last September, the Court of Appeals for the 11th Circuit unanimously ruled that businesses had the right to ban their employees from sporting dreadlocks at work. Court documents detail the undignified discourse between Chastity Jones, a Black female, and the human-resources manager offering her a job on the condition that she cut her hair. "They tend to get messy, although I'm not saying yours are, but you know what I'm talking about," she said.

Let's pretend slave masters didn't cut Black women's hair as a form of punishment; since African hair naturally locks due its texture, calling dreadlocks messy and unprofessional is calling Black hair messy and unprofessional. Yes, hair texture is not an "immutable characteristic of Black persons", as per the court ruling; but it is degrading to expect someone to alter their ethnic features in exchange for a livelihood.

According to Mintel, sales of chemical straighteners fell 12.4 percent between 2009 and 2011. The revival of the pro-Black aesthetic has had a major impact on the $185 million US Black hair-care market. Makes you wonder just how far white monopoly capital is willing to go to protect profit margins, doesn't it? They certainly own the lion's share of this lucrative market.

In Miami last July, OneUnited Bank CEO Teri Williams said African-Americans spend 1.2 trillion dollars annually, but Black-owned businesses only benefit 2 percent. "That's bigger than some countries in the world," she said. "The reality is that our community is building wealth in other communities and not amongst ourselves."

There will always be pressure to 'look the part', and get that Rolex, but surely there is a line to be draw when looking the part starts to translate as 'achieve—or rather, buy—whiteness', especially considering the beneficiaries of such a system. This conundrum gives new meaning to the term corporate slave.

"He must be able to detect no inconsistencies in slavery; he must be made to feel that slavery is right; and he can be brought to that only when he ceased to be a man."

– Frederick Douglass, continued.

NNPA NEWSWIRE (2017)

WHEN BLACK MEN FETISHISE YOUR AFRICANESS

Chapter 28

"Take me back to the Motherland," he yelled as he came, and I responded to this ridiculousness with a chuckle. It wasn't so much that I was amused, I was taken aback by the sheer ignorance of a man who literally just graduated with a doctorate degree in African Studies.

This was not the first time I've had to deal with microaggressions while dating in America...

I am South African.

Yes, I am light-skinned.

Yes, there are light-skinned Africans.

This became my usual response to conversations on dating applications since my arrival to the United States a year ago. Preconceived notions of what Africans looked like or what we sounded like always seemed to be what dominated discourse on first dates, even small talk before hook ups.

"Did you say you were from Africa?" one man I met on Grindr once asked as he led me through his backdoor, pretending I was a Mexican handyman there to fix his tabletops so the neighbors wouldn't ask questions.

However, with a *doctorate* in African Studies – and a whole thesis that focuses on the exact community that I am from in South Africa – I expected Dr Motherland to be more culturally sensitive (more woke, dare I say).

I've seen it all during my year in the Washington DC area: reluctance to give me their phone number and address fearing I might be a scammer trying to steal their identity, I've been met with suspicion because I articulate myself "so well" in English… one boyfriend even called me "savage" because of my radical politics and progressive relationship believes – because I do not subscribe to Western standards?

What is ironic about my experiences is that I've only had to deal with these types of microaggressions with African-American men, with whom I shared a history and heritage of marginalisation; yet, I remained foreign to them, even in a climate of the new renewed black consciousness.

Actually, they seemed to get their thrills from dehumanising and belittling this well-educated and established African man, here as a guest of the United States government because of his unique set of expertise. They acted like their citizen status *Trumped* all of my credentials, as though citizen status was a stamp needed for validation. It was as if they believed that I was trading dick pics for green cards – because all foreigners, apparently, are only in it for citizenship.

But, I suppose the type of shit Black gays consume in the media does nothing for the African image – *bravo*, Black Entertainment Television – with every reality star on Real Housewives of [insert random black stronghold] dating some dodgy, rich African who is funding their trips to the Caribbean, spa days and girls' night out… lifestyles, even.

One time, for kicks, I sent a picture of me playing with a lion cub at the Johannesburg Loin Park to a prospective fuck and told him it was my pet lion, Mufasa. Not only did he believe me, but he responded with, "Awwwww I want too!" – as if they sell them at the pet store down the road.

But, as much as I try to make light of it, this fetishisation of my Africaness is just irritating, to say the least. It's like dating white men who "live for big Black cock" – come to think of it, someone once said that the only thing Black about me was my cock. In fact, everything I have mentioned thus far could have easily come from those white men who pervert Blackness.

Are African-American men the white men of Black men? Maybe, maybe not. But for as long as they keep expecting us to hop off the plane looking like Eddie Murphy in *Coming to America*, they are surely as ignorant as them.

HUFFINGTON POST (2018)

COMING TO AMERICA AS PUBLIC ENEMY #1

Chapter 29

"Just don't go there and be gay, Angie," says my grandma to me as I tell her about all the things I will do when I trek to the greatest country in the world: The Land of the Free.

I am not surprised; in fact, we've had this conversation a million times before. As an LGBTQ rights activist in Africa, you are never really safe, especially not in the rural settings I sometimes find myself in. Grandma is always worried about my safety; I am her favourite, after all.

What strikes me about it this time is that I am not relocating to rural, outright homophobic Africa. I am moving to one of the greatest and supposedly most liberal countries in the world; and, her concerns for my safety are just as valid.

In trigger-happy America, ending up dead because someone thinks a certain way about you is, evidently, as simple as walking to the corner store for a pack of Skittles.

The Orlando nightclub massacre that left 49 dead sent shock

waves through the world; it sent a care message to the rest of us that the United States, the so-called beacon of democracy, was riddled with conservative terror akin to all those nations it spent years occupying for the sake of liberty.

And add to that regular reports of police brutality and unjust killings of Americans of African descent and an intensified sentiment of Islamophobia.

"You should cut your hair. Then you won't look like a Muslim," my friends would say about what they called my Jew-fro. "But, then you'll look Mexican and they will deport you. Donald Trump is going to build a wall, you know."

I'd brush off their concerns as silly banter; Americans were not going to vote that idiot into power, they're not that dumb. I honestly believed that as a guest of the state department, I was safe from the type of violence we saw regularly—that is, until I was called into the embassy for a briefing on my year-long fellowship in Washington DC.

"This is your DS-2019 form. These are your immigration papers. Have them on you at all times," says the official handling my paperwork and travel arrangements.

"Like, in my wallet? You're joking, right?" I ask.

"I would at least keep a copy on me to be safe; you don't want any problems," she responds.

For the first time, it dawns on me: I am officially an immigrant in the US. I am a gay immigrant… who is Black…and looks Middle Eastern—or Muslim, to the average American. I am Public Enemy Number 1!

I quickly set up an appointment with my hairstylist and

said goodbye to my curly locks. I scanned and emailed my immigration papers to relatives and friends and lawyers "just to be safe." I packed my bags strictly to airline regulations and ended up at the airport.

Sure, I had legit immigration papers and you would think this would offer some form of protection. But what was I going to do—use them as a shield against bullets in the crossfire between EuroAmericans (and those institutions protecting their interests) and everybody else?

Police reports document the execution of 512 Black people by police officers in the US since the beginning of 2015, according to *The Guardian's* online tracking tool. While the police killings of EuroAmericans are much higher than this, the proportion of African-Americans killed by police matched to the total population is more than double that of EuroAmericans.

I blame police bias against people of color in the US on inflammatory, and more often than not, derogatory rhetoric thrown around, dressed as freedom of speech. Public support of dangerous racist and xenophobic attitudes by presidential candidates is a prime example of this. Responsible leaders are meant to support social cohesion, not fuel an already toxic situation.

My country, South Africa, also comes from an apartheid past and has placed human dignity as a top priority in our Constitution for the sake of reparation. An important feature of our Constitution is legislation that makes discrimination based on race, gender, sexual orientation, and disability illegal; this includes hate crimes such as hate speech.

Our government realised very early on that protecting people's right to dignity is the only road to social cohesion, as it offers universal protection to all, especially minority groups, at every level of society.

Yes, people may not respect the right to dignity of many groups in society; but, the laws in place allow for recourse in instances where parties are negatively affected by the actions, and even utterances, of others. It also makes people wary of the things they say and, in effect, affects the social perceptions of certain groups, because toxic attitudes have no space to fester in the public realm.

But, what do I know? I am just an immigrant from Africa—a gay immigrant, if you're my grandma. I'll just keep my fingers crossed and throw some bones every time I leave the house and hope my African ancestors are with me as I brave this concrete jungle.

TAGG MAGAZINE (2016)

TRUMP-SIGNED AND PROUD

Chapter 30

What an amazing time it was! I arrived in the United States capital on the eve of an election that seemed sure to culminate in its first female president. The polls looked promising and the prospect of another meaningful democratic victory bore a sense of endless possibility.

Electricity filled Washington DC; it was intoxicating. The idea that by the end of my fellowship I would be awarded a certificate by the American government, signed by Hillary Clinton herself, excited me for the prospects that would follow – it seemed second best only to one signed, Barack Obama.

The scramble that soon followed, to convince the outgoing president to sign our certificates before vacating the White House was, then, rather ironic – a futile attempt to salvage the merit of our accolade. But we had to follow protocol, and protocol dictated that the sitting president sign off on all awards. That president: reality TV personality, Donald Trump.

Never mind the fact that he was as credible as a Kardashian, the hateful rhetoric that defined his campaign for presidency – particularly against immigrants – and the widespread violence against people of colour that soon followed his victory made this a very bitter pill to swallow.

As an African immigrant that looked Middle Eastern, I was already quite shaken by the incidents of police brutality that flooded my social media timelines. I was assured that I would be safe on campus, but, like the president and caliber thereof, things soon changed.

The discovery of a noose at nearby university was the first sign of this, followed by another at a fraternity house *on* campus. Then, a black (recent) graduate who served in the US army was murdered by a fellow white student at the same campus bus stop that I used every day.

Everything changed. Power-crazed white people picked fights with random strangers in public. Anything progressive became an alternative fact. If you were not "red" or red in the face, you had a target on your back – and the gunman leading this hunt was citizen No. 1.

On a mission to flex his newly acquired muscle, Trump began to make ludicrous changes to foreign policy. Along with his announcement of a "Muslim ban" and plans to proceed with construction of his infamous wall, news began to surface that he would cut funding of educational diplomatic programmes such as the Fulbright Fellowship, of which some of the world's greatest leaders are alumni.

Acquiring this prestigious fellowship was not child's play; it took years of hard work and sacrifice, and here Trump was reducing it to a handout for poor third world countries.

We started to hear about delays in certificate delivery at

other universities, who were forced to proceed with graduation ceremonies without the necessary documents. There was no guarantee that we would ever receive them. The White House could not commit to a deadline – and one didn't have to think too hard as to why.

Sure, nobody could dismiss that we had completed this amazing feat as some kind of alternative fact. In fact, I can't imagine anyone being asked to present certified copies as proof given the impressive track records participants already had. However, that someone so unqualified could simply decide to take something so special away just because he felt like it, was deflating.

But he signed, eventually; every last certificate awarded to representatives from every "s***hole" on the planet. His orange face probably turned red, having no choice but endorse those whom he loathes.

His menacing signature, which looks ready to bite and suck the blood out of your veins, is a reminder of what I've been able to accomplish despite the hostility. It also reminds me that justice can and does prevail for those who dare to fight for it.

THE SUNDAY TIMES (2018)

AN OSCAR FOR THE MARGINALISED

Chapter 31

"This goes out to all those Black and brown boys and girls and non-gender-conforming [people] who don't see themselves."
— Tarell Alvin McCraney, accepting the 2017 adapted screenplay Oscar for "Moonlight" with Barry Jenkins.

The 2017 Oscars was as politically charged as expected. From host Jimmy Kimmel's mocking of the president during his opening monologue to Ava DuVernay's conscious decision to wear a gown by a Lebanese designer, a multitude of A-listers used the 89th Academy Awards' platform to highlight injustice promoted by the Trump administration's foreign and domestic policies.

But the biggest demonstration against Trump's regime was not found in the blue ribbons many celebrities wore in support of the American Civil Liberties union; it was in the seemingly miraculous best picture victory of the underdog "Moonlight," a movie representing those often shunted to the margins of society: Black and LGBTQ Americans. The fact that the win was originally handed to "La La Land," a film that glorified old, white Hollywood, then rescinded after the mistake was realised, added to the unreality of it all — and the symbolism of the achievement.

"Moonlight" was to the Oscars what marginalised communities are to American society: minorities struggling for place in a social structure carefully designed to exclude them from participation. "La La Land," on the other hand, is white privilege personified. It grossed $140.9 million in the month since nominations were announced in late January, while the low-budget coming of age story about a young Black man growing up in Miami raked in a total of $1.5 million at the box office.

This David and Goliath battle became a metaphor for the current political climate in the United States, where a white majority voted for a party representing policies skewed against minority groups in apparent reaction to their progress in recent years.

For some of us, the Oscars was the presidential election all over again, and we waited with baited breath to see if white America would make the right choice this time around. If "La La Land" walked away with the Oscar for best picture this year, it meant that white supremacy extended far beyond Middle America, where Trump's core constituency is based, and that efforts to diversify Hollywood are just for show — along with the supposed protections afforded to all by the American Constitution.

All through his election campaign, Trump signaled his intolerance toward "Black and brown boys and girls and non-gender-conforming" individuals. Then, within a few weeks of assuming office, he proved his rhetoric was more than just speech-making, having signed an immigration ban and revoking inclusive public school guidelines regarding transgender bathroom rights.

With a bill granting US citizens the liberty to discriminate based on their religious beliefs in the pipeline and consistent calls for Mexico's president to fund a wall barring access to the United States, the Trump administration is evidently dead set on its mission to disenfranchise the LGBTQ community and people of colour.

Hence, this Oscar win is very much for those Black and brown boys and girls and non-gender-conforming individuals dealing with the consequences of bigotry, hysteria and misinformation — or what the *New York Times* would call "lies." It says to them their lives and their stories may not fit the razzle-dazzle template of Hollywood, America's key cultural export, but that they are equally important and worth telling. In short: Their lives matter.

This demonstration went far beyond placards and calls for action — it was action; it was progress in light of all the regressive policies proposed by the White House. It was, perhaps, the beacon of light needed in trying times for the American people.

THE BALTIMORE SUN (2017)

#WOMENSMARCH: IS THE MESSAGE LOUD ENOUGH FOR TRUMP?

Chapter 32

"First they ignore you. Then they ridicule you. And then they attack you and want to burn you. And then they build monuments to you."

Often credited to Mahatma Gandhi, the above quote actually stems from trade unionist Nicholas Klein's 1918 address to the Amalgamated Clothing Workers of America in Baltimore. His address came at the height of, now, much celebrated protest action opposing conservative labour policies in the US.

Well over a century later, this very country finds itself rife with activism opposing not just the regressive politics of the newly elected presidency, but the president himself. Nationwide, many have taken to the streets since Donald Trump was elected into the White House desperately trying to halt the reversal of progress made under the Obama administration.

Cynics question the point of protest after the fact, insinuating that it is too late for real impact since the new administration is well in its legal right to govern the country as per the agenda it set out during its campaign for office. They don't seem to understand that democratic participation extends beyond the ballot paper and that protest plays a crucial part in the balance of power in any democratic society.

The Women's March on Washington, which took place on 21 January, is reported to have been the biggest demonstration in US history. If the estimate by crowd scientists quoted in *New York Times* is anything to go by, then over 450, 000 people showed up to the nation's capital alone, never mind the hundreds of thousands who showed up at 'sister marches' in other major cities.

"A Metro official said that more than a million rail trips were taken Saturday, the second-highest day in its history after Barack Obama's first inauguration in 2009," it reported, contrary to what the Trump administration would like us to believe about attendance of his inauguration outnumbering both aforementioned events.

Its mandate, as per the march's official website, was simple: "The Women's March on Washington will send a bold message to our new government on their first day in office, and to the world that women's rights are human rights. We stand together, recognising that defending the most marginalised among us is defending all of us."

It employed the age-old strategy of mass action to make sure concerns about plans to cut back funding of sexual and reproductive healthcare, and disregard Obama's transgender bathroom decree, as well as disparities in wages between men and women in the country.

"In the spirit of democracy and honouring the champions of

human rights, dignity, and justice who have come before us, we join in diversity to show our presence in numbers too great to ignore."

You see, these protestors understand something that the cynics do not: the power of disruption.

With hundreds of thousands of people crowding the streets at your workplace, good luck making it to your desk on time, good luck getting through meetings with the buzz of chanting right outside your window, and good luck trying to get lunch.

Protests are disruptive so that you have no choice but to engage. A demonstration like the one witnessed on Saturday is literally that: a demonstration of power to disrupt, as well as the extent of this disruption. Such a disruption in the productivity of a city like Washington DC could have grave consequences for the entire nation. Even if Trump decided to work off site, not many others would have that luxury.

In South Africa, we are all too familiar with this, with the value of our currency plummeting at the simple threat of disruption to productivity. We witnessed this when nationwide student protests calling for free education broke out in 2015; and again, when protests calling for our president to resign erupted two months later.

At that point, when a demonstration begins to have a ripple effect, the issue consequently begins to affect more than just protestors in the street. Everyone becomes affected by the matter and everyone benefits from its resolution, and everyone calls for a resolution to be met.

There are already plans to intensify protest action over the next 100 days, leading up to a second march in April, since the Trump administration seems undeterred with the signing of an executive action on Monday, barring international non-governmental organisations supporting abortion from receiving US funding.

However, as the protest becomes louder, it will be harder for the government to ignore. In the words of renowned Australian anti-nuclear activist Helen Caldicott, "Sometimes it's appropriate to scream at them," especially when talking falls on deaf ears.

THE DAILY VOX (2017)

NATIONAL BLACK HIV/AIDS AWARENESS DAY: IGNORING FACTS, FUELLING STIGMA, AND SPREADING HIV

Chapter 33

Those of us working in HIV prevention have always believed that the spread of the virus was largely due to stigma around sex and sexuality, and that the only time we'd see any sort of difference was when society started engaging on the matter more openly. But, it wasn't until the 2009 report on the correlation between the spread of HIV and stigma in the Dominican Republic that we could claim it as a fact.

The implications of this report illustrated how social attitudes create an environment which propels the spread of HIV: stigma affected treatment toward people living with HIV; this has consequences for access to sexual health services and the way they are administered by health professionals, or rather, denied; stigma consequently affected at risk individuals' willingness to seek HIV-related services, including testing. Stigma, therefore, drove the spread of this virus.

This is evident when observing the prevalence of HIV among African-American women in the United States (US). According to the Centers for Disease Control and Prevention (CDC), of all women diagnosed with HIV in 2014, most new infections were attributed to heterosexual sex and an estimated 62% of women diagnosed were African-American.

CDC attributes this trend to the fact that "the greater number of people living with HIV (prevalence) in African-American and Hispanic/Latino communities and the fact that people tend to have sex with partners of the same race/ethnicity". New infections among injectable drug users, both men and women, were relatively low.

What this implies is that somewhere along the line, the men these women are having heterosexual sex with, are having unprotected sex with other men. Because if HIV prevalence among African-Americans is showing an increasing risk among Black women, and Black men who sleep with men remain most affected by the virus, then there are heterosexual men sleeping with men.

While the LGBTQ community has made massive legal strides in the US in recent years, religious condemnation of same-sex relationships remains rife. Religion continues to be a cornerstone in African-American communities as it played a significant role in the liberation of Black people. Faith-based leaders often site the spread of HIV among the greater African-American population to support anti-gay rhetoric.

This misinformation breeds stigma, creating an environment where people are scared to engage the matter beyond the pulpit. They are not discussing facts; and the fact of the matter is, according to a 2005 study, sex with a partner who had a history of incarceration was a key driver of HIV infections among newly diagnosed African-American women.

A 2002 review of HIV in US prisons states that in 1997, there were less than 35,000 inmates living with the virus on any given day; and that in the same year, just under 150,000 of those released had HIV. Infection among inmates in prisons is more than five times greater than the rate among people who were not incarcerated, according to the CDC. Yet, HIV-prevention interventions in prisons are limited to testing and treatment.

Those of us who believed that stigma around sex and sexuality drove the spread of HIV were right; that's what the facts showed. But, even with facts staring us in the face, we continue to let hysterics dictate our response to the pandemic.

THE MTV STAYING ALIVE FOUNDATION (2017)

IF SEX BETWEEN MEN HAPPENS IN PRISON, WHY NOT OUTSIDE?

Chapter 34

Criminals are (arguably) the ballsiest lot of the male human species. Their veins are said to stand erect with testosterone – in fact, they probably sweat the stuff. Their blatant disregard for rules places them above any other law-abiding man on society's hierarchy of manliness.

I mean, the true measure of a man is his ability to do whatever the hell he wants. No rules!

These types of men think they're invincible. They spend months – years even – living like the world belongs to them. They're the man, they're invincible. Until they get busted and sentenced to many years in prison. Bummer.

So it's bye bye unlimited amounts of stolen cash. Farewell to the endless stream of women. Bye bye booze and drugs. Hello burnt pap, iron bars and Brokeback Mountain-style sex.

For as long as I can remember, any hint of homosexual behaviour made one less of a man. That's the reason my caterer mother never taught me how to cook. The kitchen was not my place as a man. I was yelled at for talking with my hands, making friends with girls and, a lot later in life, kissing boys (by the way, I liked it – eat your heart out Katy Perry!).

Now, I know there's this whole theory behind man-to-man sex in jail, and in mining hostels and other such places where men spend days on end with other men. It goes something like this: Men have sex with men within such settings because of the testosterone flowing through their veins which increases their libido and (due to the absence of females) they end up releasing all of their sexual energy among themselves.

Apparently this is not gay behaviour.

In that case, call me Queen Elizabeth. I'm sorry, but having sex with a man is having sex with a man. It is homosexual intercourse; it's as gay as Elton John. Finished.

A 2001 Wits University study found that sex between men in Southern African prisons is very common. It also noted that long term sexual relationships between prisoners are normal. It's still hard to digest though, the whole "jailhouse rock" thing and how it is any different than sex between men outside jail.

It hit home one day when my father went off on a homophobic tangent. I said to him, "Oh please, man. They used to *naai* you in your bum when you were in jail. You just think you're so much better."

My thoroughly annoyed father, who had been in prison for five years, looked at me and replied, "You must get your facts straight. Nobody *naaied* me, I *naa . . .*"

He didn't finish his sentence and didn't need to. Besides, I didn't believe him anyway. The fact that he'd had gay sex didn't shock me so much as his idea that because he was on the "giving" end of these sexual encounters it made his behaviour less gay. It was as though he was saying: I was still the "man."

The man? Please, if I am a sissy for sleeping with men, then he is one too – and so is every guy who's ever had sexual thoughts about other men, or acted on those thoughts.

But it isn't having sex with another man that makes him a sissy, it's the fact he was not able to own up to it. I couldn't stand that he pretended that another man did not sexually excite him. Why was he suddenly ashamed? I mean, what ever happened to the real man who did what he pleased no matter what anyone said or thought?

What happened to that man with no respect for the rules or the norms – not to mention the law? What happened to that man? Or rather: that "man."

As men, we are taught to be proud and brave. We are taught (incorrectly) that the world is ours. We are made to believe that anything we do is okay. So why isn't it okay for me or any other man to be attracted to men? I am a man. I choose to act on my impulses and to sleep with other men. Why should I feel ashamed? And yes, I'll admit it; I sometimes do.

Is it religion or society or biology or a mixture of all of the above? Or is it that all the out sissies (including me) are too scared to man up? Either way, I have a feeling that daddy dearest and I have a lot more in common than either of us would like to admit.

GENDERLINKS (2012)

I'M COLOURED, NOT A CAVEMAN

Chapter 35

I was taken aback – to say the least – when I stumbled across a comment piece on the Independent Online website focusing on the death of a Newlands East teenager, Montreal King.

The young soccer enthusiast was stabbed to death in front of hundreds of people during a fight at a Durban Day event earlier this month. The piece by budding comedian Carvin Goldstone tried to unpack the teen's tragic death in an effort to highlight the widespread violence in marginal communities; but, while his intentions were probably from a good place, the manner in which he addressed the issue probably caused more harm to the community he is trying to service than good... however, I believe that he is not the one at fault here; the newspaper that published his piece is.

I spent most of last week discussing the situation with colleagues; Goldstone's generalisations about Coloured people, culture and communities were unfair, unfounded and simply reinforced negative stereotypes. The title, "Don't f*** with me,

I'm Coloured", already positions the Coloured individual as someone who is temperamental, confrontational and brash.

Goldstone, known for his family-friendly accounts of growing up in the eThekwini township, admittedly never uses vulgarity in his shows; so, why choose to lace this particular reflection on a community with f-bombs and close relatives if not to reinforce popular (negative) perceptions of it? "You may know me for my comedy show, No Swearing," he writes, "so I will mind my language in this piece as I attempt to drive home some ideas and points in a very brash and at times vulgar way."

Don't get me wrong, the comedian made some valid points in his account; and I agree with him, Coloured people have been backed into a corner: economically, politically and socially. And yes, this may very well be the reason why the number of violent crimes is high in these predominantly Coloured townships; but, this issue is not specific to Coloured communities, all marginal communities face high levels of violent crimes. The driving force behind these crimes is poverty, not race or culture.

Goldstone goes on to say that violence is something Coloured people are taught by their parents, who encourage them to display macho tendencies as a tactical defence mechanism for this marginal group. "I call it Coloured bravado," he writes. "It manifests itself at the lowest and highest levels of Coloured life. I've seen it on the school playground and in boardrooms. It's the feeling that because we are Coloured, we must not back down from a fight."

What made me uncomfortable was not Goldstone's observation about the use and threat of violence as a desperate measure for power and influence, but that he insisted it was something that was specifically Coloured. "For Indian, white and Black people living in KZN, [King's death] was a disturbing window into a reality of Durban's Coloured community," he writes.

The bravado that Goldstone refers to is not a Coloured thing; take me for example: while I am part Coloured and part Indian, it was my Indian mother who always insisted that I stand my ground when I was a child. Bravado is not even a Black thing, nor is it a class thing; whole wars have been fought over clashes in ideology – think World War I and II. In patriarchal societies, all men are taught to stand their ground, to defend and protect, to be warriors. Goldstone's observation is, therefore, unfair.

I am aware that the comedian wrote from a point of view informed by his personal experiences, and as a man who identifies as Coloured, was pleading with a community he has a vested interest in to reflect on King's death and resolve to address the issue of violence. However, the newspaper's readership consisted of all races that read his column and shaped their understanding of this community around what he put forward.

For those who already believe in some of these stereotypes, Goldstone has just validated their prejudices. That's how stereotypes work, and that's why it is unethical to perpetuate them in the media. Stereotypes are dangerous as they can – for starters – demotivate a particular faction of society from aspiring to be anything but what they are told they are. Secondly, they are dangerous because in shaping people's impression of a particular group; you also influence their attitudes toward that group. Stereotypes are not good for social cohesion and the use of stereotypes in any setting (actually) is unprofessional.

Although he is not a professional writer, Goldstone comes from a journalism background and should have a basic understanding of the journalistic code of ethics in South Africa. Assuming that he does not, the newspaper it was published in does. "The views expressed here are not necessarily those of Independent Media," reads the disclaimer at the end of the article in an effort to remove the publication from any responsibility. However, the newspaper is not obligated to publish every submission made and should apply its editorial policies to all content it chooses to publish.

They were, evidently, uneasy about what Goldstone had to say and they should have consulted with the comedian so that his piece addressed this burning issue without framing an entire community in a negative light. They would have avoided this ethical dilemma they are faced with; and perhaps then, would it have been better received and achieved the results Goldstone presumably hoped for.

As a media practitioner, I am all too aware of the lack of representation of the Coloured community in mainstream media.

So, I commend Goldstone for taking the time to try and get the conversation started; but, it is unfortunate that responses to the piece have been around his positioning of the community and not about addressing violent crimes and the culture of violence.

A simple browse through the comments section displays resistance from Coloured readers around his alleged "self-hate" and racist attacks from non-Coloured readers who are using this space to advance their own agendas. Yes, Goldstone's got the country talking; but a little bit of editorial discretion would have inspired a very different conversation.

NEWS24 (2015)

NEWTOWN "MOFFIE" MURALS: HYPERMASCULINITY & HATE SPEECH

Chapter 36

While thousands celebrated the Constitutional grains of LGBTQ people at Johannesburg Pride this weekend, just down the road, a toxic battle brewing between graffiti artists continued to any other: I was running a bit late for work, I grabbed my lunchbox off the backseat and proceeded to the front door of our Newtown office. As I opened the door, I glanced back to see if anyone was behind me and went cold; across the road from my work place stood graffiti all over the wall of an abandoned building which read, "PLEASE NO MOFFIES".

This is not the first time I've seen graffiti like this in the area; on the very next block, on a pillar holding up the M1 highway near the entrance of Newtown Junction, *"DON'T BE A MOFFIE"* reads under a mural in glaring black and yellow paint.

When I first saw it, I wasn't sure what to make of it. I tried not to make a fuss in the name of artistic freedom, convincing myself that the artist was being sarcastic or trying to make a point of sort about patriarchy in South Africa. But, the emergence of a second mural only justifies my uneasiness about the first; I had no business trying to legitimise the use of hate speech in the public domain.

As an advocate for LGBTQ rights, I know very well the consequences of letting attacks on the community slide; and we have come way too far – legally, anyways – to allow such degradation.

Just last month, another video made rounds on social media showing a group of school children assaulting a male classmate. Speaking to the *Weekend Argus*, the pupil's father said that, leading up to the assault: "My son has been called a *moffie*. He is much smaller than the other kids and hangs out with girls."

Also in recent months, *The Citizen* exposed hate speech by several conservative Afrikaaners on social media who claimed that "moffies" were to blame for natural disasters in the world, and more specifically in Knysna. According to one bigot, runaway fires which left six people dead, were apparently the wrath of God being meted out on a town that had shown far too much tolerance towards homosexuality and gay weddings.

With every new "moffie" mural or tag – and there have been several since – it is becoming clearer that at the helm of this whole debacle is tiff between rival graffiti artists, as many of the newer ones sought to deface existing artwork in the area.

Graffiti has a history in the reclamation of public space by marginalised urban communities. However, this callous display of hypermasculinity, which is deeply rooted in hip hop culture, has no place in a society that strives to remedy the symptoms of patriarchy. We cannot give play-play gangsters hyped up trap music bravado the room to act out these toxic displays.

When City of Joburg mayor Herman Mashaba introduced bylaws restricting the production of street art last year, graffiti artists accused his administration of not differentiating between gang graffiti and legal graffiti productions – their proverbial bread and butter. However, in this case, hate speech infringing on the constitutional rights of LGBTQ individuals, are present in both commissioned work and incidents of vandalism.

Graffiti murals are an integral part of the aesthetic that is Newtown; they once masked urban decay caused by corporate's exodus from downtown Joburg in the '90s – and are a drawcard in its increasing gentrification. One looks forward to seeing new work which showcases an incredible amount of skill and talent; however, artists have begun to play a very dangerous game by throwing around homophobic slurs on the walls of our economic hub.

Thousands of people travel in and out of the city daily, allowing this rhetoric to grace our walls endorses violence against LGBTQ people – because this in itself is a form of violence.

I don't, however, believe that new bylaws are a solution to the problem, since we already have pretty clear laws around the right to dignity enjoyed by every citizen in our country – including an outlaw on hate speech. What is needed is for authorities to enforce these laws, which is pretty much the song LGBTQ activists have sung with every new legal victory overlooked by society.

THE DAILY VOX (2017)

HOW THE CLIMATE CRISIS IS PERPETUATING HATE CRIMES IN SOUTH AFRICA

Chapter 37

An ignorance of our core constitutional principles often reverts them back to their age-old value systems as a gauge of morality. And within many of these cultures, people like me are not only condemned to the bowels of hell, but are seen as a symptom and a sign of the end times — as per the religious text 86% of South Africans claim to subscribe to: The Holy Bible.

Coupled with the devastation that the climate crisis is wreaking on the world, let alone the African continent, ring-winged rhetoric and religious dogma have steered blame away from the greedy colonial corporations pillaging the Earth to those bearing the proverbial scarlet letter of progressiveness (that many have been led to believe these religious texts warn us about).

The real culprits of these seemingly biblical droughts, floods and locust infestations are cooped up in their corner offices in far off lands, away from the public's gaze. The sheer spatial design of our townships keep the majority of poor South Africans far away from the displays of opulence in the leafy, almost exclusively white suburbs.

It is the so-called "wayward" members of society, who live down the road in our ghettos, that have become easy and attainable targets for retribution. We've become sacrificial lambs in our communities' efforts to save the world.

Recently, research by the Intergovernmental Panel on Climate Change's (IPCC) confirmed that the Southern African region was already experiencing climate changes that are more rapid, and with impacts that are more severe, than the global average.

But we don't need a report to tell us that; over the past two years, locust infestations we observed in East Africa now plague our agricultural provinces, droughts have dried up our taps in some parts, while severe floodings have claimed countless lives in others. (All of this, while the Covid-19 pandemic relentlessly tore families apart.)

During this time, we also saw an unprecedented number of hate crimes perpetrated against members of the LGBTQIA + community — including the brutal murders of 20 gender-nonconforming individuals. The surge of violence against LGBTQIA+ people prompted President Cyril Ramaphosa to publicly denounce the attacks and prioritise new protective legislation.

Slow-onset climate change impacts, like water scarcity, lower crop and ecosystem productivity, are forcing people to migrate in search of opportunities elsewhere in a country where the climate crisis is fast shrinking what little opportunity is left to find.

The impact of climate change on our food security is already apparent; the cost of food has skyrocketed in tandem with the rate of unemployment and poverty in our country. An estimated 40% of South Africans go to bed hungry — a figure that will certainly rise as the impact of the Russian war on Ukraine compounds exiting food injustice across the continent.

And if South Africans cannot afford food, they certainly cannot afford to go to university – one of the only places to formally learn about climate change in our educational system. Also, there is still a large portion of our population without access to the internet. This means that millions of South Africans rely on these personal networks and communities to make sense of what is happening (and as already established, the vast majority of them belong to faith-based communities).

Hunger often leaves people vulnerable to manipulation by the powerful — and religion has long been used as a means to sustain systems of exploitation across the continent. It makes sense that so many people are misguidedly seeking redemption in an era defined by fear mongering, instead of challenging the root of their deprivation: the *real* reason we may very well face the end.

Without effective sensitisation of the climate crisis in grassroots communities, historically marginalised groups such as the LGBTQIA+ community not only remain at risk of violence, but will continue to be systematically excluded from our failing economy, as well as relief efforts aimed at alleviating climate impacts.

"When the people shall have nothing more to eat, they will eat the rich," philosopher Jean-Jacques Rousseau famously said. Yet, history has shown us time and again that it is society's most vulnerable who are thrown out to the wolves — for reason often gives way to hunger pains, and my people are starving.

DAILY MAVERICK (2022)

A SOUTH AFRICAN REFLECTION ON TYONNE JOHNS

Chapter 38

A year has passed since the senseless murder of lesbian chef and business owner Tyonne Johns, who was stabbed to death over a conflict involving a pile of folding chairs. This is what official reports of her death will have you believe, anyway. However, her friends and family have a very different account of the 35-year-old's killing: they believe the attack was motivated by homophobia. They believe her death was a hate crime.

I cannot claim to know very much about the vulnerabilities of black lesbians in the United States; in fact, the only account of hate crimes against lesbians in America I can recall is the 1999 film *Boys Don't Cry*, in which Hillary Swank earned an Academy Award for her portrayal of a masculine-of-center lesbian who is raped and murdered.

However, as a South African, narratives of brutal attacks on lesbians—particularly black lesbians—are all too familiar.

World-renowned photographer and activist Zanele Muholi made waves when she first documented the inhumane practice of "corrective rape" in South African townships (ghettos) in a 2003 exhibition capturing the stories of twelve survivors called The Rose Has Thorns.

At the time, Muholi was quoted to have claimed the motive for these attacks on masculine-of-center lesbians was to "turn you into a real African woman" and to "cure" them of homosexuality.

Since then, many other cases have come to light, with a Cape Town support group claiming to handle an average of ten new attacks per week in 2009. But even with all the evidence laid out in front of them, the South African Justice Department refused to acknowledge these attacks for what they were: hate crimes.

Year in and year out, men would stand trial for brutal attacks, merely sentenced to between ten to 20 years when found guilty of MURDER. Families just happy to see any conviction at all talk to the media, overwhelmed by the victory, that they don't really process how small it is in relation to their loss.

Then came a momentous ruling in 2013, aiming to send a message out to these bigots that their offences would not be tolerated: the man who raped Cape Town lesbian Millicent Gaika was sentenced to 22 years in jail.

This ruling spelled out what our justice department tried hard to sweep under the rug in fear of the whirlwind it would ignite within the legal system—because of populist attitudes, perhaps, or maybe the lack of will to offer a bit more protection for a group so vulnerable. But, one cannot stop a storm: late last year, South Africa green-lit a Hate Crime and Hate Speech Bill, which will hold perpetrators to task long before hatred can escalate to violence.

A law is no silver bullet to the end of hatred toward LGBTQ people; what's on paper doesn't automatically filter down to the ground. It cannot turn patriarchy on its head overnight. It certainly isn't going to stop sticks and stones being hurled at black lesbians daily. It does, however, give them grounds for recourse and respect for their dignity—because when bigots are made to pay for the life they destroy with whatever is left of theirs, then only are they able to see its worth.

TAGG MAGAZINE (2017)

ANNOYING, OBSCENE, AND DANGEROUS: STRAIGHT GIRLS WHO LIKE GAY CLUBS

Chapter 39

"OH MY GOD!!!! I LOVE YOU GUYS!!! I LOVE DICK! YOU LOVE DICK! WE ALL LOVE DICK!!!!" screams a Kardashian wannabe at a group of gay men lining up outside a new Los Angeles queer space I recently visited called Queen Kong.

Everyone on the sidewalk stares at the raving (shitfaced) lunatic – we're conditioned to immediately pay attention to screaming white girls – and then stares back the group of men she's yelling at as soon as what she's broadcasting clicks: ALL THE MEN STANDING HERE LOVE DICK!!!!

I have not felt so exposed, vulnerable, and frightened since the day a group of my straight male high school friends "jokingly" held me down and tried to take off my pants so they could give me "what I liked."

I've heard a lot about "annoying white girls" who have made a trend of interrupting queer (safe) spaces with their drunken, obnoxious antics; but, as someone with a female best friend for the past 25 years, I have always welcomed women into our (safe) spaces because they don't really have any of their own. My best friend loves to dance, and it certainly puts my mind at ease knowing that she is less likely to be drugged and raped in the process at a club where hardly anyone is interested in her.

I've always brushed off silly banter – you know, the "If you weren't gay..." microaggressions – as a good time, letting down of hair and walls and social standards. However, when your presence starts to make me feel scared for my life, it's time for you to go.

You think I'm just being dramatic? Just under a year ago, we saw one of the largest massacres of LGBTQ people in history right here in the so-called "Land of the Free," the west, flagship of democracy. In fact, that the Trump administration was voted into power should serve as a clear indication that progressive and liberal attitudes remain with a minority – geographically and politically, anyways.

So, whether SHE loves us or not (as a straight person) it doesn't mean that everyone else on that busy Downtown L.A. street does.

Couple attitudes of intolerance with American's (ironically) liberal gun laws, and I am justified to feel I am only one extremist away from Orlando Shooting 2.0 right there on the sidewalk – and for what? Because some sloppy drunk decides to publicise my sexual orientation without my consent?

No tearful "I'm super sorry" or special commemorative emoji

is going to make up for the potential loss of my life, so use whatever brain capacity you have left and SHUT THE FUCK UP, O-M-G!

She might find it fun and funny sounding like the Oprah of dick loving on this seedy sidewalk, but we're all nervously smiling while watching our backs, hoping her Uber driver will arrive soon and take her back to a straight club. Straight girls have become to gay men what straight men are to them: annoying, obscene, and dangerous.

TAGG MAGAZINE (2017)

COLOURED MAN RUNNING IN THE SUBURBS

Chapter 40

The jacaranda trees along the avenue were in full bloom, the street covered in purple blossoms – it was simply spectacular. I had noticed it quite a few times on my way to work and, being an aspirant slay kween, decided I would take a picture for the 'gram on a day I wore my favourite outfit.

The day had arrived and on my way home, I pulled off on the side of this quiet road a few blocks from my house: no cars, nobody walking in the distance, just me in my designer treads walking to-and-fro the camera phone set on auto capture.

After a while, the owner of the house where my car is parked pulls up in an SUV, watches me for a while and proceeds into the yard. No biggie. I was almost done; in fact, I was pretty sure I caught the money shot 10 minutes before. As I began to pack up my stuff, another car pulled up in the driveway – I assumed her husband. He rang the intercom and without a "hello" a quivering voice on the other side asked: "Are you okay?"

Are you okay?!

Why wouldn't he be?

Oh wait, there was a strange Coloured man standing outside your house.

Let's just pretend that in the five or so minutes she spent watching me that she didn't see me take photos of myself; did I look like I was dressed to rob or hijack white people in the suburbs? Because the last I checked, hijackers wore Uzzi hoodies, not Zara shirts.

Did she really miss my new iPhone sitting on the specially ordered, paid-way-too-much-in-duties tripod in front of me? Surely, she looked out the window if she wasn't sure. I mean, she would have realised that I wasn't so much of a threat the moment she made it into her home without incident, right?

Nope.

All she saw was a Coloured criminal ready to do something bad to her.

This is not the first instance I've been mistaken (to put it lightly) for a criminal by white people in my neighbourhood. I jog every day. I take the same route. I start my jog at the exact same time. Yet, every time I am out for my daily run, one of the neighbours (perhaps the same one each time) calls the security company to follow me around.

I am sick to death of being policed in places I pay good money to live in – ironically, by the same security company that I am subscribed to. Being one of the few Coloured people on the block, surely they would remember my face. I cannot believe I have to constantly justify my presence in the land of my ancestors to the same criminals who stole it from them.

You end up smiling and waving off every ADT car that stalks you around the block to show that you're not there to cause trouble. It irks you and you take it to social media, but you don't risk being gunned down with the pump action shotguns that these boys have been dying to play with. (Hell, you even buy reflective running shorts to make sure you don't look like a fleeing burglar).

But, no matter what you earn or own, the number of degrees you have up on your wall, or the level of *twanglish* you speak, it only adds to the suspicious minds of suburbanites who then assume you're just another corrupt BEE businessman – read as a crook.

What they don't get is that I didn't choose to join the apartheid-era trend of migrant labour for myself. Quite frankly, it is not my fault that all the economic opportunities are in the north; selfish white business owners pulled out of the CBD at the end of apartheid to cause its collapse.

To be honest, I would much rather live where I grew up, surrounded by good food, good vibes and people with good manners – you know, the type that greet their neighbours, not call the cops on them as if we still live in *1980-voetsek*.

But, this is the reality I have to navigate, and no amount of what-could-have-been is ever going to change it. I suppose I'll just have to soldier through my daily jogs until it finally scares my racist neighbours off to one of those gated estates – transformation will come one way or another.

THE DAILY VOX (2018)

WILL THE LAND EVER BE RETURNED, AND DIGNITY RESTORED?

Chapter 41

"**L**ook, Tony! They've put up a wall – it's beautiful," my grandmother says, dragging her words to match the slow pace of the car as we pass by our old family home near Sophiatown, Johannesburg.

I have never seen the inside of this house; in fact, my father wasn't even born when the apartheid government moved my family to a nearby "Coloured" township. But, we have driven past on countless occasions; each time, my grandmother marvels at every renovation and paint job, as if its current owners were simply minding it for her.

The mass dispossession of land experienced by my community during the implementation of the Group Areas Act in 1959 – which saw the formalisation of racially segregated ghettos in South Africa – was certainly not the first, nor would it be the last.

The Bleek-Lloyd Archive entered into Unesco's Memory of

the World Register documents, through extensive personal accounts, the violent forced migration of so-called Khoi-San people into the country's western interior long before the arrival of colonial powers.

Award-winning anti-apartheid journalist Sylvia Vollenhoven notes, from her study of the 12,000-page journal, an era in which "settlers and other Africans were intent on the complete destruction of (these) people; they were driven off their land, their languages were banned and they were enslaved".

This is by no means an exaggeration. When the Khoekhoe and San retaliated against Dutch settlement at the Cape of Good Hope in 1652, they were declared vermin and systematically hunted down by invaders, who were given strict orders to shoot them dead on sight.

"In 1660 at a conference in the Netherlands, Jan van Riebeeck submitted a report, stating that these people (Khoi-San) came and claimed their land," former Minister of Rural Development and Land Reform Gugile Nkwinti acknowledged in a recent public statement, to contextualise the communities' drawn-out struggle for their ancestral land.

My community's history is a painful one, akin to that of many other first peoples taken captive within their borders. And, just like the histories of other indigenous populations globally, has been manipulated to serve those lusting for control of the land and its natural riches.

One such account, a familiar, outdated narrative, in which local chiefs surrendered land to colonists in exchange for alcohol, re-emerged in public discourse as debates around land reform raged in our Parliament. This myth, once the cornerstone of colonial expansion, continues to damn my community into chronic marginalisation.

Last year, our courts ruled against arbitrary farm evictions without alternative shelter in order to end an age-old practice of leaving farm workers who are unfit for work displaced – predominantly pensioners who have spent all of their lives working the fields, and those left disabled by work-related accidents.

Not even a month had passed after the hearing when the South African Human Rights Commission reported a spike in illegal evictions in Western Cape, a so-called Coloured stronghold. Over a hundred people were expelled from land they've spent their entire lives tilling, forced into shacks in nearby shantytowns like their ancestors.

The monumental parliamentary vote in favour of amending our Constitution to allow government expropriation of land without compensation may be just the answer to restoring dignity to a community pushed to the margins for over 300 years.

"We are saying people who are landless but who work the land must own it," said the ruling party's economic transformation head, Enoch Godongwana, after President Cyril Ramaphosa announced the motion in Parliament earlier this year.

As it stands, our Constitution blocks indigenous people from the current land reform programme because of a 1913 cut-off date – the year that the Land Act was adopted. This prevents restoration of any land stolen before then: land belonging to the Khoekhoe and San, some of the most valuable land in South Africa.

Consequently, their descendants are condemned to the mold-ridden walls of the same rotting public housing, in drug-infested neighborhoods, designed by the apartheid government to disenfranchise them.

Apartheid members of Parliament would pump narcotics into Coloured neighborhoods by smuggling them in the undercarriage of delivery vehicles, writes Dr Don Pinnock in his 2016 book documenting gang culture in Cape Town, Western Cape.

The honorary research associate at the Centre of Criminology at the University of Cape Town's reflection on the city's deep class divide perfectly captures the extent of which the community has been ostracised:

"Foreigners lounging on palm-lined Camps Bay beach gazing at the steep mountains framed by gossamer clouds would find it hard to imagine that shoot-outs, drug wars and human trafficking were taking place a few kilometres from where they sit."

About two years ago, news stories emerged of 23-member families living in tiny two-bedroomed apartments, when violent protests broke out in several Coloured ghettos. The situation was explosive, prompting former president Jacob Zuma to meet residents in Eldorado Park, a township neighbouring Soweto.

Their main grievance: systematic blockages to adequate housing and the land to build it on.

Residents fed up with illegal land grabs on adjacent government-owned plots, which were promised to them during election campaigning, believed that the failure of our government to protect their interests placed the community in a crippling choke hold.

Leading up to the protests, Dr Blair Proctor of Michigan State University's African Studies Department conducted extensive research in Westbury, an equally neglected Coloured neighborhood close to Johannesburg city centre. He notes in his 2016 dissertation:

"Former politically-radical Coloureds feel betrayed by the (ruling party) for not acknowledging their plight and essentially maintaining them within a marginalised and intermediate space of ambiguity."

The numbers support the communities' cries; the 2017 SA Poverty Trends Report reflects an accelerated rate of poverty within Coloured communities as compared to other race groups, having experienced a 4.2 increase in percentage points matched to the 1.8 increase experienced by other African populations.

The South African Human Rights Commission recently released its findings from a national series of hearings to gauge the human rights situation faced by South Africa's first people. It found in conclusion that:

"...although (Khoekhoe and San) form only a small portion of the poor in the country, their dire situation is exacerbated by multiple factors including a pervasive negative stigma, social exclusion, a declining culture, a lack of official recognition by the state, and a muted political voice."

The commission stated that access to land was of paramount importance to indigenous peoples, as the historic and ongoing dispossession of land removed their means of sustenance, giving rise to impoverishment.

South Africa stands a turning point where it can truly address the injustices of the past.

Our government's decision to give our country's most vulnerable communities a stake in the land that they have lost, but continued to service, will afford them greater protection from exploitation and a legacy to lift future generations out of poverty. But, most importantly, it will begin to restore the dignity they were stripped of.

In due time, they won't have to look out car windows, marveling at land that was once theirs.

DAILY MAVERICK (2018)

SMALL-SCALE FISHERS' HERITAGE IS SYSTEMICALLY GUTTED

Chapter 42

Boats in every colour of the rainbow rock gently as the tide comes in on the chillingly quiet harbour. When I first visited here in my youth, the market was as vibrant as the boats docked along its piers, banter and laughter were a distraction from the fishy stench that stung the nose; but now, there's not much distraction from the fast-spreading rot.

People are always perplexed by what is happening on the Cape Flats – plagued with gang violence, an illegal narcotic pandemic, as well as disproportionate rates of intimate partner violence. But, what they never seem to understand is how so much of deterioration is due to systemic issues that start at the top – and how many of these ghettos were once thriving communities.

Harmful industrial fishing over the past three decades has had a trickle-down effect that has forced many of these coastal communities into illegal fishing activities since they do not have the permits to fish legally. This had tainted perceptions of local fishers, swaying local support of small-scale fishers, and further marginalising them.

What is clear from our conversations with the fishing communities is that people are losing their birthright due to unfair laws that are preventing them from carrying on their age-old tradition of small-scale commercial fishing – causing unemployment and stripping away the communities' means to sustain themselves.

"You will find that over a period of 30 years, the community is involved in these illegal activities, and they are criminalised based on the law that does not allow them to access the [fish] in the area that they are living in," said Professor Moenieba Isaacs, Academic Coordinator at the Institute for Poverty, Land and Agrarian Studies at the University of the Western Cape.

Instead of prospering under the country's democratic regime, three decades of corruption under the new South African dispensation has led to a collapse of our fisheries, and the communities they once employed.

"They say you mustn't lose your culture; but the way that things have gone, they've taken Kalk Bay's culture away. They took away fishing," said Moegamat Alie Fortune, an 85-year-old, fourth-generation fisher from Kalk Bay.

Fortune explained one of the key challenges faced by small-scale fishers was that they struggled to obtain licenses from the government due to the stringent requirements by the government, which most fishers, due to the informality of their businesses, fail to meet.

He described the knowledge that the gatekeepers of fishing

licenses have of the nature of fishing in the Western Cape as "dangerous".

But, while small-scale fishers are battling for fishing permits, harmful industrial fishing companies continue to destroy and deplete the country's marine resources. In fact, our laws are actually favourable to the industrialisation of fishing in South Africa.

Ferial Davids, who cleans fish at the Kalk Bay fish market, said that there has been a drastic decline in the number of fish local fishers are bringing in. She suspects that it is a result of trawling along the Western Cape coastline.

"It's not a lot of fish around now lately. I suppose it's because of the big trawlers that are around. There used to be hundreds and hundreds of snoeks here on the harbour; but nowadays, it's like ten snoek, 20 snoek, not even a hundred snoek for the day," she said.

On Mandela Day, Minister of Environment, Forestry and Fisheries Barbara Creecy announced that they would begin granting 15-year licenses to small-scale fishers for the first time in our country's history. Responding to the cries of the community, she committed to rolling this out as early as October.

However, the fishing community remains skeptical, as the bottlenecks they continue to encounter are right down to the administrative level.

Our country's small-scale fishers aren't alone in their struggles; recent media reports exposed how the Senegalese government continued to grant licenses to foreign vessels these last years despite barring their local fishers from operating and how fishmeal industries are threatening jobs of women fish processors and food security of millions of people.

Prof Isaacs warns that the trend of industrialisation in the fishing sector across Africa will have a catastrophic economic impact, especially on those most vulnerable:

"90% of the continent's fishing activity is small-scale, and a majority of the people who are on the shore base are women that are either selling, drying or salting the fish. There is a big incentive for governments of the African continent to formalise the rights of small-scale fisheries."

THE SUNDAY TIMES (2020)

BIG OIL'S GENERATIONAL CURSE: POLLUTANT-RELATED EPIGENETIC CHANGES KEEPS SOUTH AFRICANS IN POVERTY CYCLE

Chapter 43

Not much has changed in the 40 years since Shareeza Domingo's family moved out of Wentworth.

It is a Saturday morning and the streets are beginning to buzz with children's voices as they prepare to partake in soccer fixtures scheduled around the neighbourhood. Even those who don't play for official school teams at the sporting grounds opposite Engen's rotting refinery are putting together teams for tournaments at makeshift pitches next to its infamous flats. Aunty Kat is already seated at her spot in the shade of an adjacent tree, where she spends her days waving at passersby.

Wentworth is certainly one of those South African townships where everyone knows everyone else.

Former resident Shareeza Domingo recalls a typical weekend in the neighbourhood during her youth: "There was little to be done in the 1970s, I would say. Basically, it would be a trip to town to do your shopping, get back and the kids were all in the road and everyone was playing, parents are braaing and having time together."

Shareeza's fond memories of her childhood neighbourhood prompted her to show her daughters, Lamise and Mahira, where both of their parents were born and raised. Having lived in the northern part of Durban since 1992, she felt it important to give them a sense of where their family was rooted, a community she always speaks of with tremendous pride.

It was exactly how she remembered it to be: the way it looked, sounded and felt. The community still finds joy even in its hardship. But just a few moments into their excursion, Shareeza quickly remembers the real reason they had packed up their four-bedroom home in exchange for a small apartment in Durban's central business district: "the smell" that killed her father.

"When we entered Wentworth my two girls said to me: 'Wow, y'all had to live in that smell? That smell that's stinting? I can't breathe.' My eldest one's father is also from Wentworth, and he also had asthma. She also has asthma, and kept saying, 'I'm choking, I'm choking.' So, we just left."

Wentworth, situated in the South Durban Basin, is surrounded by nearly 300 petrochemical industries, with over 150 smokestacks. Formalised under the Group Areas Act during the apartheid regime, its population is still predominantly Coloured.

Much like other so-called Coloured communities across South Africa, this community continues to spiral into economic despair despite the country's hard earned democracy. But, unlike other townships in the north of Durban with similar racial compositions, one of the key drivers of poverty experienced here is the elevated rates of illness due to long-term exposure to air pollution created by the surrounding industries.

"Although children both in the north and the south were affected by the pollution, the children in the south had much more asthma than the children in the north," says Professor Rajen Naidoo, an epidemiologist and head of occupational and environmental health at the University of KwaZulu-Natal.

The University of KwaZulu-Natal's groundbreaking research into the impact of air pollution on the South Durban community began 20 years ago, when residents reported alarming numbers of pupils losing consciousness at school.

"Work really started with a single school, the Settlers' Primary School. There was an incident where a large number of children were collapsing and it was attributed to the elevated levels of pollution in the area," explains Naidoo.

"Settlers' Primary was a very interesting school. If you stand out in the playing fields of that school, if you look out in the one direction, you see the smokestacks of the Engen refinery. If you turn around, directly behind you, you see the smokestacks of the SAPREF refinery [Shell and BP]. So clearly depending on which direction the wind blew on a particular day, that school was always in the middle of it."

It was then when they discovered that the area was indeed a cancer cluster, with leukemia rates in children under the age of 10 at least 24 times higher than the national average — but continued study of the community revealed a more dire situation.

"We hypothesized that it is possible that there is something that genetically reshapes children such that they become more susceptible to develop asthma, because historically we know that asthma is a genetics-based disease," adds Naidoo.

"It seems likely that the pollutants are causing what we refer to as an epigenetic change over a shorter period of time within generations… and that it is still likely that the next generation or two will still be carrying some of the pollutant-related burden going into the future."

It is, then, not surprising that despite their move out of Wentworth even before her daughter's birth, Shareeza's eldest daughter suffers from asthma today — just like her father.

"People thought, 'It's in the genes.' They'd say: 'So, the father had asthma, it follows the same genes. Of course the child will follow.' That's what people would say. They knew that the oil refinery was a hazard, but how do you prove that?"

While the Domingo family were able to move out of Wentworth, for most of the residents of the South Durban Basin, there is no refuge from the highly polluted neighbourhood. Naidoo explained that when the lion's share of an already marginal income is rationed toward the healthcare needs of chronically ill children, there is nearly nothing left to help families escape this toxic environment.

"A lot of the people have been staying there for three or four generations because they are not able to step out. Parents build their children so that they can move up into the next level and escape that poverty cycle, but they are not able to do that in South Durban."

"Our young people are suffering worse off than ever before. Not only is there a double-dose of asthma, cancer and leukemia, but they don't have money to study further," said veteran environmental justice activist and co-ordinator of the South Durban Community Environmental Alliance (SDCEA) Desmond D'Sa.

D'sa's mission to protect his community's constitutional right to a healthy environment earned him the 2014 Goldman Prize. His family was dismantled by the Group Areas Act when he was a child — with only some of his siblings moved to Wentworth, while others were placed in other racially-based neighbourhoods.

He co-founded the environmental movement in Durban in response to the large number of injuries and deaths experienced by workers at the refineries due to the toxicity of their work environment. D'sa says that not only are these oil giants evading responsibility for the suffering they have and continue to cause, but they are also further disenfranchising the community through their discriminatory employment practices.

"Engen doesn't have a habit of employing budding engineers from the community. In fact, they don't employ our skilled people here because they know through the medical assessments that they do that already people are affected with their health. So why would they employ people from here?"

Soaring unemployment rates in the community, coupled with the mounting financial burdens created by chronic health issues, has had a toxic knock-on effect on the social fabric of

Wentworth.

"A sense of hopelessness comes in when a person is unemployed, and those frustrations obviously get carried out and are seen visibly within the community through the abuse of substance, physical violence and the manipulation within your own personal relations," says Oliver Meth, a gender-based violence activist from Wentworth.

In 2002, Meth was brutally raped by a group of young men in his community. He was just 16. When he had approached the police to report the crime, he was ridiculed and turned away. This hate crime was later used as a case study when the South African government was forced to expand its Sexual Offences Act to include all forms of nonconsensual sexual penetration regardless of gender as rape.

His story is but one example of the lack of institutional support in the community, as well as the extremely high levels of gender-based violence in Wentworth. Meth believed that the only way this community can rid itself of the worst social symptoms of systemic inequality that plague it is to create more economic opportunities for its residents.

"The main struggle for them is that people are thinking about the immediate, like to put food on the table, and not the long term consequences that these refineries pose to them. The long term effect is not as important to them for now because they are just trying to get through the day," adds Meth.

Currently, there are very few opportunities available outside of these toxic industries, and what little opportunity remains continues to be threatened by the fossil fuel industry. While these oil giants have all announced their plans to finally abandon these rotting refineries, several more are scrambling for drilling rights along the Southern African coastline.

With firsthand knowledge of the exploits of big oil, local fishers and Indigenous Peoples groups fight tirelessly in court to prevent any further loss to their livelihoods because of greedy, colonial industries. Corporations that continue to take advantage of countries in the global majority whose environmental laws are less strict than in the countries these multinationals are headquartered in, according to Naidoo.

"We've got to, firstly, have a situation where polluters accept responsibility for what they are doing and what they have done in the past. We've got to have a government which holds those polluters responsible, make sure they understand what they've done and put into place plans that redress that," says Naidoo.

"And yes, it can be done. If these companies have been generating massive amounts of profits for all these years, then now, it's in a sense, payback time. You've exploited these communities. You've exploited these environments. Now, you've got to make good."

"We don't want these big corporations running away from the country. We want them to be held accountable for people's health, and also to be held accountable for the workers," adds D'sa.

"The oil refineries robbed a lot of them of their livelihoods, their families and their loved ones. To find a way to resolve that is rather late but go back and see what you've done to the people and rectify it. Compensate them, but money doesn't save it, at the end of the day," concludes Domingo.

MAIL & GUARDIAN (2022)

BEING BLACK-ISH

Chapter 44

I am noticeably Black anywhere else in the world except Southern Africa. I've been told on many occasions that my rounded nose is a feature that is specific to Black people.

It always amuses me when people abroad try to spot the parts of me that they perceive as Black. See, they're not referring to Blackness in the political sense; to them, Blackness is interchangeable with Africaness, and speaks directly to being of African descent. And, though I am light-skinned with hair that appears straight depending on its length, I could never blend in – or dare I say, pass for white – because of my nose, evidently.

Blair Proctor of Michigan State University goes into great lengths to explain this in his 2016 comparative study of South African Coloureds and creoles of colour in Louisiana, and parallels in their relationship with Blackness.

He writes: "... the opposite of whiteness or non-whiteness: everyone that was rejected from the inclusion of western norms and ideals, were designated into the pariah of Blackness."

It is easy to spot blackness in comparison to whiteness because when one does not exactly meet the expectation of what is perceived to be white – norms and ideals. This is visibly clear even in the most "colour-blind" of societies...

In a 2015 in-depth feature on racism in the world's most diverse nation, Brazil, journalist and author Stephanie Nolen notes an innominate bias toward people who are darker in complexion.

"It is the cornerstone of national identity that Brazil is racially mixed – more than any country on Earth, Brazilians say. Much less discussed, but equally visible – in every restaurant full of white patrons and Black waiters, in every high rise where the Black doorman points a Black visitor toward the service elevator – is the pervasive racial inequality," she writes.

"Blackness" is tangible. It seems to stay with you no matter which neighbourhood you moved to or which school you attend, and it certainly stays with you no matter how you have been socialised.

In 2011, *The Sunday Times* published a feature of Black South Africans who had been adopted and raised by white families. Almost all interviewees reported feeling displaced in their new surroundings and being isolated by other children in school.

"I was growing up in a white environment. I was a brat. I didn't learn Tswana; I didn't want to learn it. The rules of the school did not allow us to speak vernacular languages... I wasn't comfortable in my body. There would be a lot of talking behind my back. Some people would say to me 'Rosie, you think you're white'," said actress Rosie Motene.

But within the binaries of race, Blackness, like whiteness, can be just as exclusive. Blackness comes with its own set of ideals or parameters which become an uncomfortable fit for those who stray further along the spectrum. This is perfectly highlighted by the social ostracisation faced by people living with albinism.

A 2010 *UNCUT* magazine article explored the stigma faced by people born with the condition due to myths around everything ranging from ill luck to organ harvesting. A sound engineer who was born with the condition, Siphon Hlophe, lamented about the difficulty he experienced trying to come by employment opportunities.

"I'd ask why because I don't believe there's anything different about me except my skin is light and my dreads are a bit blonde... People can have their own perceptions of you before you get a chance to prove otherwise."

Part of my amusement around the game of "spot the difference" non-Africans play when trying to decipher my genetic make-up is the irony that those racially classified as Black in Southern Africa struggle to see this Blackness everyone else keeps looking for.

Associate Professor Siren Pillay from the Centre for Humanities Research at the University of Western Cape states that race categorisation is to blame for the polarisation of those classified Coloured in South Africa to the broader indigenous population.

Pillay believes the term had stripped this population of its indigenous status, while other indigenous populations were categorised as native. While the premise of his argument is valid, he does not take into account the complexity of collective consciousness resulting from this polarisation.

In her 1895 explanation of the word 'negro', historian Grace King, talks about how the term was used to distinguish African-Americans who were noticeably dark from those of mixed descent in post-Civil War Louisiana.

"'The pure-blooded African was never called colored (sic), but always Negro.' The *GENS de couleur*, colored (sic) people, were always a class apart, separated from a superior to the Negro, ennobled were it only by one drop white blood in their veins... to the white, all Africans who were not of pure blood were *gens de couleur*."

When the United States institutionally changed the racial category colored [sic] to mean all people of African descent, it forced the community to develop a single consciousness and identity, despite its genetic and cultural diversity: "the one drop rule".

And while the parameters of what is considered being Black has had a profound impact on how the world understands blackness, the perpetuation of apartheid racial categories in South Africa maintains this divide between the descendants of the khoekhoe and other indigenous groups.

Professor Pumla Dineo Gqola, Dean of Research at the University of Fort Hare, believes that ideas of non-racialism are important to social cohesion and unity, but that it is premature to eradicate race from our new radical vocabularies in talks of transformation.

"Just because we have started to engage in discourse around the nonexistence of race doesn't mean that the institutional impact of race is not felt, our experiences over 400 years have made a non-existent thing tangible," she said at a dialogue on race relations in South Africa.

However, it is ludicrous to presume that South Africa lacks the sophistication needed to measure social progress outside of these apartheid categories, and that multiple schemes cannot run concurrently in the pursuit of social redress.

In fact, broadening the matrix of social indicators to include pre-colonial identities may just help deepen our understanding of social disparities and allow for more targeted interventions, instead of the current blanket approach to transformation which has allowed room for abuse.

Debates about my blackness, or even lack of it, will remain a popular discussion at dinner parties and political rallies for as long as my community is left roaming this no man's land of racial ambiguity – that is, until what I truly am has yet to make its way onto government census forms.

(2023)

LAZY ECONOMIC POLICIES WILL PERPETUATE POVERTY AMONG COLOUREDS

Chapter 45

"**O**ur country requires an economy that can meet the needs of all our economic citizens – our people and their enterprises – in a sustainable manner. This will only be possible if our economy builds on the full potential of all persons and communities across the length and breadth of this country."

– the Department of Trade and Industry.

In 2010, amendments to the Employment Equity Act proposed the introduction of national demographics to impose a setting racial targets. Addressing the concerns of what this meant for minorities that were regionally concentrated, then director general of labour, Jimmy Manyi, said Coloureds were "over-concentrated" in the Western Cape and should move elsewhere if they wanted work.

His chauvinist proposal of an apartheid-style migrant labour system, where lazy governance trumped the constitutional rights of South African citizens, was met with fierce criticism. Former finance minister, Trevor Manuel, accused him of "worst-order" racism, akin to that of apartheid's key architect, Hendrik Verwoerd.

Notwithstanding the backlash, the government proceeded with their plan through revised black economic empowerment (BEE) codes of good practice – that took effect on 1 May 2015.

Amendments to the BEE codes required for Economically Active Population (EAP) statistics to be reported under race groups that distinguish between Africans, Coloureds, and Indians; and placed a cap on the number of BEE points attainable for senior, middle, and junior management based on these race groupings.

"This matters because so-called 'Coloured' people make up 52% of the EAP in the Western Cape, but only 11% of the national EAP. Similarly, Indians make up 11% of the EAP in KwaZulu-Natal, but only 3% of the national one," stated the South African Institute of Race Relations in response to the amendments.

Employment statistics for the Western Cape, at the time, already demonstrated that Coloureds were underrepresented in the workforce based on regional data, accounting for a mere 36,6% of those employed in both permanent and temporary jobs. They also demonstrated a gross underrepresentation in management roles at all levels based on regional and national EAP figures.

The absence of prescribed regional EAP consideration in the government's current methodology means that Coloureds in the Western Cape would have a harder time acquiring management positions, and an even harder time ending poverty experienced by Coloured people.

Early last year, Statistician-General Pali Lehohla warned that South Africa faced a "cocktail of disasters" as a disproportionate number of black and Coloured youth remained unemployed, correlating with figures demonstrating that the two population groups had the worst higher education attainment.

The report, which assessed the vulnerability of South African youth, found that youth unemployment was strongly linked to those who had not completed matric, with 57% without a job, compared to an unemployment rate of 38% among those who had completed matric. It assessed the lack of textbooks, being a contributing factor to poor matriculation rates, and found the Western Cape fairing the worst (3%) in terms of the number of pupils who did not receive textbooks at all.

Schools systematically underfunded during apartheid remain well below standard. Coupled with a host of other structural barriers such as the fact that in poor households, income earners are financially responsible for at least 2.65 other people – compared to wealthy households where the ratio is one is to one – and the increasing social divide remains eminent.

Recent findings by Studies in Poverty and Inequality Institute on the right to work in South Africa suggest that while unemployment rates grew across all race groups over the past year, the most significant increase in unemployment rates was among Coloureds, standing at 1.5%. Coloureds also experienced the highest increase in unemployment rates over the past decade.

The latest Stats SA poverty trend analysis demonstrated an increase in people living below the upper-bound poverty line for only Coloured and black South Africans between 2011 and

2015. The Poverty Trends in South Africa report highlighted an increase of 4.2 and 1.8 percentage points, respectively, noting an accelerated rate of poverty among Coloureds.

The same report showed a substantial decrease in poverty rates among Indian South Africans, with poverty among white people remaining below 1% during that period. This comes as no surprise considering the overrepresentation of both population groups in top management positions, as well as higher rates of educational attainment.

Limiting access to management job opportunities in Western Cape based on national EPA benchmarks will have a devastating effect on its Coloured majority. As demonstrated, access to better employment opportunities is crucial if we are to tackle existing poverty cycles.

The intricacies of social disparities in South Africa must be considered in policy making – especially when these policies aim to transform a social system designed to create such divisions. After all, BB-BEE is meant to redress social inequality caused by apartheid, not perpetuate it.

HUFFINGTON POST (2017)

HAD IT NOT BEEN FOR B.E.E.

Chapter 46

I came under fire for publishing a piece on how new BB-BEE codes of good practice had detrimental implications for Coloured people in the Western Cape. Ironically, the very next week, Mandla Mandela publicly criticised efforts in KwaZulu-Natal to exclude Coloured and Indian people from certain BEE tenders.

I would like to make it clear that, in light of the obvious misunderstanding of the point I was making, I am not opposed to affirmative action policies. On the contrary, I believe that they could be more sophisticated to truly achieve fair access to economic opportunities without forcing people into migrant labour – provincial quotas, for instance.

Without affirmative action policies in place, there would be little to no change in the composition of the labour force in corporate SA. That there still exists such an overrepresentation of white people in the private sector, one can only imagine what it would be like had our government not intervened… let alone the types of jobs we'd still be confined to.

The fact of the matter is that I may have never got my foot in the door had these policies not existed in the first place. BEE helped identify the underrepresentation of Coloured professionals in my field that afforded me the opportunity to specialise, and then thrive in an industry that was literally instrumental in the white supremacist agenda – in other words, not meant for me.

It's like BEE literally ring-fenced that position for me. That's not to say that I was given some sort of hand out – I was qualified but not quite the devil they knew. BEE swung favour back into my court.

I became very aware of just how important my racial categorisation was in my employability a few years later when trying to change jobs.

I had responded to a number of advertised positions, but despite my qualifications and ample professional experience, I received not one response. (Not to sound big-headed, but my curriculum vitae boasts performance graphs and exclusive professional networks, never mind the qualifications and awards.)

Frustrated, I vented to a colleague, completely bewildered as to why I was constantly overlooked. To which she responded, have you indicated your race/economic empowerment status?

I didn't.

I didn't think it would matter considering my credentials. I have always taken pride in the idea that my work spoke for itself. I suddenly remembered how former editor of *The Star*, Raymond Louw, once said I would struggle to make it in the media industry because of my surname – because I had an Afrikaans (traditionally white) surname.

I wasted no time adding "EE: Coloured" to the top of my CV – and no more than a month passed before I was learning the dial code for my new, better paying, better everything, job.

I suppose it may seem really unfair that I would be given preference over a white guy with the same credentials as me, but the truth is that white people still get preference for jobs over Black professionals, with fewer credentials – mind you.

So, despite what some people believe about BEE being reverse racism, a way of inverting the hierarchical pyramid of apartheid, the numbers say otherwise. White people are not struggling to find jobs, in fact, hardly any white professionals sit unemployed after finishing their tertiary studies.

Coloured people, on the other hand, remain grossly underrepresented at all levels in the workplace – public and private, regionally and nationally. Even in the Western Cape, surprisingly. Limiting this community from management positions as per the new national quotas is counterproductive.

Public policy is not static or set in stone. It is our duty to actively participate in all aspects of society – be it in the workplace or in shaping policies that govern the workplace.

(2023)

A LIFE AMOUNTING TO PEANUT BUTTER?

Chapter 47

The driver weaves through Sandton rush hour traffic as fast as the cars in front of him allow and I fixate on what I ate today as they swish past the passenger window – not as a distraction, but as a measure of my life as it quickly draws to an end.

I had an apple at 11am, and a peanut butter sandwich at lunch – on brown. That's it, I think.

Growing up, I always imagined that magazine editors met with sources at fancy restaurants during their lunch breaks – to negotiate exclusives and pitch cover concepts. But since I achieved editorship, just before my 26th birthday, all I find time to eat at lunch are peanut butter sandwiches – two slices of bread with a swoosh of the chunky kind in-between.

My colleagues think I am obsessed; but actually, I don't even taste it until 4pm when I am burping peanut butter while suffering with such bad heartburn because of it. But my days end later and later, and I find myself snacking on peanut butter straight out the jar a lot more frequently. I hate it.

As we pull up at Morningside Clinic, and I tell the nurse about my sudden chest pains, I ask myself: was it really worth it? Every late night and family function missed? Each failed relationship, and now this: my imminent death? And, all for what? A fucking peanut butter sandwich?

(2023)

WHEN DID I BECOME A WHITE MAN?

Chapter 48

When we dream about our futures, we never quite get into the specifics of how our lives will change. We can only imagine the privileges that a good life comes with; but because we never see it firsthand, we are hardly ever prepared for it when it actually happens.

As a child, I would tiptoe barefoot across a back alley covered in a kaleidoscope of broken glass from the beer bottles my father and his friends smoked mandrax in. Seeing him and his posse cough up lumps of yellow gill as he'd reach into his pocket for the two bob I'd always asked for, was as normal to me as seeing your uncles gathered around a smoky *braai*.

This was what 4-year-old me knew; it was what I was used to. I had no other point of reference to decipher that this was a highly toxic and harmful environment.

These days, the closest I get to broken beer bottles are the pieces of green sea glass I collect on exotic beaches I visited all over the world. The only time I see grown men cough up anything is when seated in the waiting room of my Sandton doctor. And, the only thing toxic about my environment are my hostile white neighbours clinging to the past.

When I think about how vastly things have changed from when I was a chubby little Coloured boy living in Bosmont backrooms, it baffles me at what point I had acquired the privileges I grew up believing were only for white men – things I had never aspired to.

Dare I ask: when exactly did I turn into one?

When did I become this person that prefers to sit at wall tables of fancy restaurants, and then demand to see the manager when there aren't any available? At what point did I start writing to franchise headquarters, reporting my disappointment in eve-ry-thin-g that they do, and then take to Twitter when they don't humour me with an apology?

At some point, my opinion started to matter. Somewhere along the line, society started to bend its rules for me; and I found myself on the other side of the velvet rope, waving away options and opportunities served on a silver platter.

Mortgage loan offers, job and investment opportunities, Bitcoin presentations and red-carpet event invitations flood my email inbox daily; and sometimes go straight to spam. I have far too many options than I have time for, to be honest. My peers marvel at my life on social media, and I am stuck trying to make sense of it all.

But not everyone got the memo about my transition, it seems. Some mistake my caramel skin for a prison of disenfranchisement, a disqualifier of sorts, a weakness. They're quick to try and send me back to where I came from; but, I always remind them that where I am matters so much more.

They are never ready for the next-tax-bracket *twang* and Wits-graduate English that comes out of the mouth of this beige body.

Don't get me wrong, I have no delusions of grandeur. Like many other people of colour who have attained any level of privilege, I am well aware that it can be stripped away as quickly as this upward mobility occurred. I spend my days brainstorming how to avoid being three paychecks away from moving back to the ghetto, and slowly seem to be making progress.

It's not so much that I fear losing the intoxicating power that my new found social status brings, it's just such a good feeling to be treated with the same amount of respect as our white counterparts. To be able to live with that type of dignity is what our forefather not only dreamt of, but sacrificed their lives for.

'White-man respect', I feel, is the benchmark of humanity; where your presence is never questioned but appreciated, and people take what you say as gospel instead of trying to test, challenge and undermine you. It is easier, and a lot less time consuming, not having to constantly explain yourself.

I know that every time my nieces and nephews see me on television, relaying my professional opinion to clueless white presenters, it empowers them with the belief that they can contribute equally to those conversations they are often excluded from, and that their opinions can carry just as much weight as the old white men who've dominated this space for most of history.

Times have changed; not just for me. I've become a catalyst of the 'new South Africa'; the embodiment of our constitutional dream. I never imagined the role I would play in reimagining our social order. I never thought I was *that* important.

WHO SAID AFRICANS DON'T CARE ABOUT THE ENVIRONMENT?

Chapter 49

"**I** owe my being to the hills and the valleys, the mountains and the glades, the rivers, the deserts, the trees, the flowers, the seas and the ever-changing seasons that define the face of our native land."

– Former president Thabo Mbeki, 1996.

The idea that Black people don't care about the environment and that environmentalists are pushing a Western agenda in Africa is utter hogwash.

It is a cooked-up narrative that plays on racial tension in our country to allow massive exploitation of our natural resources for the benefit of an economic elite.

These tactics are not new; those at the frontline of the environmental struggle have always had a bad reputation, being painted as tree-hugging junkies by business people and politicians to deter others from associating with the cause.

In Africa, the narrative they use is that environmentalism is a "white people thing" and that environmental groups are pushing a Western agenda – because environmental protection has been corrupted to mean fewer jobs for Black people.

This is by virtue of the fact that these exploitative industries are massive employers of unskilled Black labour.

Positioning environmental protection as a threat to economic stability in grassroots African communities is preposterous considering that earnings from these minimum wage jobs are just table scraps compared with the wealth being stolen from right under our feet.

President Cyril Ramaphosa has time and again announced the government's intentions to grow the extractive industries, positioning them as South Africa's saving grace. The truth is that exploiting our natural resources has never enriched the lives of those whose birthright is dominion over the bountiful land.

Hardly any of the wealth from mining actually filters down into mining communities – in fact the sector employs just 5% of the country's workforce but accounts for a third of its exports. It is no wonder the poverty gap in our country widens with every new household survey.

A community called Kriel in Mpumalanga services two of the country's biggest coal power plants, yet residents do not even have electricity in their homes. Since the establishment of these plants, the community has seen a sharp increase in the number of people with asthma and deaths due to respiratory-related illnesses.

Whole communities are left destroyed and the land around them barren and polluted beyond salvation. But the plight of local communities doesn't seem to faze those looking down from their perfect Moody's rating pedestals.

Instead, our country seems to have become a market for anyone with money to spend. That nuclear energy may be back on the table is yet another case of this – how anyone would even consider nuclear energy in light of the recent Fukushima meltdown is just mind-numbing.

With all of the safer and greener energy options that exist in the world and being rolled out across the global West, it is highly suspicious that politicians continue to push this agenda. If anything, this line of outrageous decision making is the real Western agenda being pushed in our country.

As a people, we have always had a very reciprocal relationship with the environment. It is in our nature to protect our surroundings for the sustenance they have always afforded us. We've always understood the importance of a healthy natural environment to our quality of life. Anything different is what is foreign. The desire to abuse and destroy our very livelihood can be the thinking only of someone who does not have a vested interest in it.

So forget about the negativities multinationals tell you about environmentalists. Wanting to stop the degradation of your heritage does not make you some weird hippie; neither do you have to chain yourself to a tree and get arrested for doing so. What is important though is to make sure you take a stand for what is yours.

As Nobel peace prize-winning environmentalist Wangari Muta Maathai once said: "We cannot tire or give up. We owe it to the current and future generations of all species to rise up and walk."

NEWS24 (2018)

ECO-FASCISM IS RIFE IN THE CLIMATE JUSTICE SPACE

Chapter 50

"Covid is the world's way of balancing out this overpopulation," they say. "People should stop having so many babies. There are already too many people in the world, it just cannot handle the strain."

In my time with the climate justice movement, I'm sometimes left shocked and grossly offended by the ignorance, and casual racism, displayed by some of my peers in the name of saving the planet.

"Human beings are the problem, we should all die," sits right there at the top of the list.

Let me explain. They don't mean all humans when longing for this mass extermination, they mean human beings having babies at a disproportionate rate. And with a general lack of access to healthcare in the global majority, let alone access to family planning and reproductive health, they are referring to us: the black and brown people of the world that they assume are destroying it with our sex lives. (This adds a whole new dimension to the hypersexualisation of people of colour, but that's a whole other discussion altogether.)

This thinking is so rife within the movement that thought-leaders have even coined a term for it: eco-fascism. It is an ideology blaming the climate crisis on overpopulation, immigration, and over-industrialisation. According to *Vice*, eco-fascists think we could partly remedy these problems through the mass murder of refugees in Western countries. Oh, and by spaying people of colour like dogs, evidently.

The correlation between overpopulation and carbon footprint is horribly misinformed. In fact, believing that people who can barely afford to feed their families are the cause of the overconsumption that is responsible for climate change sounds pretty silly when you say it out loud. In my country, South Africa, over 50% of the population lives below the $1.90 per person per day poverty line. So, we are definitely not the ones to point a finger at.

On the contrary, our culture is not wasteful. Being of both African and Asian descent, I can almost categorically say that frugality is instilled in us – probably because there is never really much to go around in our communities. Eco-friendly practices such as reuse, meat-free meals, and subsistence farming have been a part of our culture long before they became trendy in the West.

Who you should be pointing a finger at are those so-called "developed" countries who, despite their excellent family planning facilities and controlled birth rates, contribute the most to the world's carbon emissions.

In 2015, Oxfam released a study that found that the richest

10 percent of people worldwide produced half of the planet's individual-consumption-based fossil fuel emissions, while the poorest 50 percent of the world's population – about 3,5 billion people – contributed a mere 10 percent.

Yes. The reality is that carbon emissions are predominantly caused by, and for the comfort of, the wealthy whiter West; but impacts the poorer, Black and brown people of the world at an alarmingly disproportionate rate.

A series of recent reports by the United Nations Environment Programme showed time and again that environmental injustice – from pollution, from harmful extraction, from overconsumption – are people of colour, particularly women. One study found, for example, that the differences in gender, social roles and political power in regulating plastic and health standards placed women at high risk of developing cancer and having *miscarriages*.

As noted by my fellow Fulbright award recipient and climate activist, Dr Alex Lenferna, the global economy is run on the devaluation of Black lives and Black land, often in the service of predominantly white capital and interests. Lenferna wrote that in the end, environmental injustice is in many ways an extension and continuation of colonial injustice – that is, the exploitation of our land and people to benefit former colonial powers.

The belief that people of colour are inherently to blame for everything wrong in the world is a tired and counterproductive narrative that continues to mislead people by shifting focus from the real problem, and those who are really in the wrong. There is no more room for gaslighting. And, right now, we don't have the luxury of being anything but honest with ourselves if we are to stop the crisis on our hands.

Only if we are truthful with ourselves, can we find real and effective solutions to the climate crisis, as well as the environmental injustice faced by the global majority. We can't rely on false solutions that encourage genocide and fuel hate – that is far too big a price to pay for your overindulgence.

(2023)

BROWNS' SEX-ASSAULT ADVERTISING BLUNDER SHOWED IGNORANCE

Chater 51

"**I**t wasn't my choice to be kissed. The guy just came over and grabbed! That man was very strong. I wasn't kissing him. He was kissing me."

– Greta Zimmer Friedman (2015).

The iconic "V-J Day in Times Square" photograph by Alfred Eisenstaedt portrays a US Navy sailor grabbing and kissing a stranger – a nurse in a white dress – in New York City on Victory over Japan Day 1945.

During an interview with the Library of Congress, that nurse, Greta Zimmer Friedman, recalled how the sailor overpowered her in what is probably the most famous case of sexual assault of all time.

This interview resurfaced in recent weeks as 60 women came forward with allegations of sexual harassment, sexual assault and rape against Miramax cofounder, Harvey Weinstein.

The ordeal, which inspired many other survivors of sexual misconduct to speak out about the violence they had experienced via the hashtag #MeToo, prompted a several columnists to probe into rape culture, some even reflected on Friedman's account of her widely celebrated assault.

That diamond dealer Browns opted to use this image in their latest marketing campaign, called Love's Embrace, shows utter ignorance, if not arrogance, on the part of advertisers whose top-down approach is as dated as the famous image's romantic appeal.

The advert appeared on the cover of the latest Sunday Times – ironically, right below an article about how another woman, former ANC MP Jennifer Ferguson, accused SA Football Association boss Danny Jordaan of repeatedly raping her, over 20 some odd times!

All of this within the context of gross levels of sexual violence in South Africa, with an average of 109.1 rapes recorded by the police service each day over the past year. Bear in mind that the product being advertised by the jeweler is geared toward women, the same group most affected by this type of violence.

Brands cannot afford to be this sloppy anymore. The perception that they are selling products to a bunch of consumers is ill-informed and dangerous – heck, last week's tweets about Dove's recent racist advert are still fresh on our timelines.

They need to start seeing audiences as investors who make very conscious decisions on which products and brands to buy into. There exists a massive paradigm shift in the way that people engage with products on the market because of new media technology.

As brand architect Sylvester Chauke put it: "Consumers have been freed from the chains of one-way communication since they can now compliment and condemn brands in an instant. 140 characters have become quite powerful today as we watch TV and also follow the commentary on [social media] – the world has indeed changed!"

According to Chauke, technology has liberated consumers from being captive audiences to active participants. A bad customer experience at a retail store is more likely to be addressed on social media than it is in-store. Strike the wrong nerve with a faction of society (let alone the one you're targeting!) and the entire Twitterverse will come crashing down on you.

Ever so often, a company will make headlines for firing employees, scared that the bigoted views they express on social media might have a harmful effect on the brand. THAT is the media climate we live in.

The influence social media has on what people choose to spend their money on is not overstated, nor is it unfounded. A 2014 retail study by Deloitte found that 56 percent of consumers buying baby products are influenced by social media – the number was 40 percent for home furnishings, 33 percent for health and wellness, and 32 percent for automotive.

What this means for people working in advertising is that a lot more work needs to go into it: know your audience like that back of your hand, know what makes them tick and DO NOT cross that line. Ensure that they are represented in the production process, not just present for formality sake.

Research every aspect of your creative product from the text used to the symbols you use – and of course, the images. Even the smallest detail can have the biggest impact. You do not want to be that brand that endorsed sexual assault to sell engagement rings.

HUFFINGTON POST (2017)

SPOTIFY AND R.KELLY: WE SEE YOU ON THE #METOO BANDWAGON

Chapter 52

In case you missed it, Spotify just removed R Kelly's music from its playlists to kick off its new Hate Content & Hateful Conduct Policy. This is all part of their new marketing strat... Oops! — I mean response to rising levels of gender violence.

I find it a bit opportunistic for the streaming service to publicise its decision to "ban" the singer, in pursuit of the unmissable buzz that #MeToo has created around gender-based violence. It is actually pretty distasteful that they would choose to leverage a campaign rooted in the suffering of the very people they position as beneficiaries of this move.

Every major media outlet covered the news — you couldn't pay for that type of publicity, and that's what made me wary of their actual intentions. And — thank God — I was not the only one.

Since the announcement on *Billboard*, many social justice warriors have called them out online, questioning whether Chris Brown, Eminem and Red Hot Chili Peppers' music would also be removed in light of their histories of gender violence and current criminal charges.

The streaming service has yet to respond — and while they have committed to growing their list of sanctioned artists, they have yet to indicate who is set to feature (... or rather, cease to feature).

That Kelly was their first target with this policy didn't particularly impress me. As is, the child molester's career is on a decline; he had to cancel several shows last year because of poor ticket sales. With hardly anything to lose, Kelly was low-hanging fruit.

If you are genuinely trying to be an ally to the cause, the rules are simple: you shut up and stand at the back. And you do not make it about yourself.

Chances are that they didn't anticipate what this decision meant in the greater scheme of things; how quickly the profits gained from a bit of publicity after the announcement could be outweighed by the loss of sales by sanctioned artists.

What would the financial implication be of removing someone like Eminem from its playlist? Here is an artist who remains one of the most profitable rappers of all time, who has literally killed his ex-wife in the music (several times!). Surely, he violates this policy.

I don't see them removing Tupac's music either. His cult following may paint him as a saint, but the deceased rapper served jail time for sexual violence. Shouldn't they turn the volume down on his music too? In light of this policy?

I suppose it would be foolish to do that with all the hype the recent movie and TV show is creating. There's nothing like a TV special to get people nostalgic enough to download "Dear Mama" again for the umpteenth time; in fact, his greatest hits album charted again on the Billboard Top 40 after ten whole years.

Such is the nature of the corporate machine, where profitability is all that matters — every decision is made by weighing up how much money will be lost against how much is gained.

Everyone knew about Kelly's inappropriate relationships with young girls; his penchant was never a secret — yet nobody cared enough to make an example of him when he had us all "stepping in the name of love". Because for as long as people continued to dance to his music at wedding receptions and at 3am in the club, he was untouchable.

The Kelly ban actually had the converse effect of what they were trying to achieve. The number of people streaming his music on the platform went up after the announcement.

After years of lobbying against him, women's rights groups have finally made it uncomfortable for anyone to listen to this sex predator's music in public (#MuteRKelly). People are out there questioning what listening to Kelly's music says about them and, generally, fold to the pressure. What value was Spotify hoping to add?

It wouldn't be the first corporate player trying to capitalise on the social justice bandwagon. Just look at how Kauai jumped on to #StrawsSuck, even though it is practically impossible for you to drink out of their smoothie cup without one, because of the types of cups they use. But luckily for the world, the internet quickly intervenes.

The Kelly ban actually had the converse effect of what they were trying to achieve. The number of people streaming his music on the platform went up after the announcement — something that would not have happened had they been bold enough to boot him off the streaming service completely.

Attempts by businesses to corrupt and highjack social justice campaigns are simply sickening. It's suddenly fashionable for them go "#MeToo" on every other hashtag that trends online. If you are genuinely trying to be an ally to the cause, the rules are simple: you shut up and stand at the back. And you do not make it about yourself.

HUFFINGTON POST (2018)

TRANSGENDER OR "WHATEVER"—HOW MEDIA IS FAILING THE TRANS COMMUNITY

Chapter 53

I'm taking a class in media representation of minorities (read as: marginalised communities) because, quite frankly, I am sick to death about what the media says about me as a gay South African Coloured male – the order you place these identities makes little difference to what they say about me. I decided to take this class to gain expert insight around the matter so that I, as a media creator, could proactively work on shifting the narrative and, consequently, public perceptions of who I am.

Last week, as we discussed a recent media event dealing with a transgender teen winning a court battle granting them the right to use a locker room of their choice, my lecturer blurted out: "The pronoun thing is tricky because you never know if he's a she, or whatever."

Err, no! There is nothing complicated about a journalist asking a person which gender they subscribe to; heck, we're never too shy to ask them about anything else. In fact, it is a journalist's job to ask all the necessary questions. Yet, here is a media veteran, whose apparent expertise is in reporting on minority groups, and their advice to an entire class of aspiring journalists is to do "whatever" until there is clarity out there, somewhere. This attitude is unacceptable.

It is our duty as media to take the lead on matters of social reform. The public rely on us for direction and therefore, we sure as hell need to ensure that we gather the information they require of us. Accordingly, we're meant to demonstrate to the public how to put into practice developments in society and the impact on language use – that is, "the whole pronoun thing," as the professor teaching this class put it.

(And FYI: the best practice is to ask people – whether they appear transgender or not – which pronouns they use because making assumptions about anyone based on their appearance is undignified, and just bad manners; if someone looked sad, you'd ask them about it, not make assumptions about what you think may be wrong with them.)

How will society learn to accept our trans brothers and sisters – and siblings who do not subscribe to either terms in this binary – if the media we rely on for direction can't, doesn't, or refuses to? And, while we wait for "whatever" to transpire, vulnerable communities continue to experience the worst atrocities: murders of 27 transgender people were reported last year, making it the deadliest year on record for transgender people.

Continued "or whatevering" around transgender issues influences the public to regard such human rights violations against this population as marginal, insignificant even. We're talking about a population group accounting for a million US citizens–doesn't seem so small anymore, does it?

Media completely neglects its societal role when it neglects the transgender community – so much for being the "voice of the voiceless" and "watchdog of society"! And with a whole new generation of journalists entering the newsroom with "whatever" in mind, coverage of transgender people leaves much to be desired.

TAGG MAGAZINE (2017)

TOXIC MASCULINITY AND "OBJECTIVITY" IN THE NEWSROOM

Chapter 54

I was working on a story on male corrective rape and, during that time, I had this recurring dream.

In the dream, I was in a taxi by myself. I'd see the taxi driver looking at me weirdly. I'd stare out the window and see other taxi drivers. It was scary because, if I opened the taxi door, they would come in. But if I stayed in that taxi, I would also be raped.

Either way, I was fucked.

I've never really spoken to anybody about this, especially at the time I was writing the story, because you don't want to seem overly affected by things. Especially as a journalist, I just felt as though saying I was affected by it would undermine what I was trying to expose.

Once I saw this lifeless woman on the pavement. This man had bludgeoned her to death and her brains were, like, oozing out into the drain. I remember the response from my editors. How, you know, "you're being emotional about it".

I think that has always stuck with me — not to show that I am affected by these stories because the newsroom [has] a culture that has filtered down through all these decades — that you kind of need to be cold under the guise of being "objective".

It's a terrible culture because we do stories to expose social ills. And how do you really change things if that kind of culture filters through to the newsroom, dictating the way you work? It makes what you are trying to do as a journalist kind of superficial, I think.

MAIL & GUARDIAN (2018)

REALITIES OF SOFT DISCRIMINATION

Chapter 55

A year ago, I took the Drama Queen of the Year Award, at my organisation's end of year party. While these awards were meant to be light-hearted and we all received mall vouchers and other goodies as a prize, it bothered me that I was being recognised for my so-called office antics and not the quality of my work which I have devoted so much of my life to. It also made me wonder if, as in the case of many females in the workplace, my sexuality blinded people to what I actually brought to the table.

Ever since females were allowed to hang up their aprons and join the workforce, they have been chastised for being emotional in the workplace, forming cliques and letting family responsibilities interfere with their work. This was ironic considering stereotypes of the angry boss and boy's clubs existed long before affirmative action. Common labels for females in the workplace (particularly in management) such as "b***h" and "dragon lady" not only dehumanise females by describing their work ethic as animalistic, they are also evidently gendered. Other examples of gender discrimination, probably more popular in the '80s, include the labeling of corporate females as lesbian. It is on this premise that I argue terms such as "drama queen" within a professional setting are derogatory as one's work ethic is undermined because of your sexual orientation or preference.

In my case, to put things into perspective, I single-handedly improved the quality and frequency of the publication I manage on the smallest budget we have ever had in the history of the magazine. My work on this project and numerous other side projects earned me a Young Leader Runner-Up Award at the 2014 Nelson Mandela Community Leadership Awards, an event recognising excellence in leadership in Gauteng – and attended by provincial premier David Makhura. None of my triumphs would have been possible had I not hounded down our finance department to pay suppliers (which almost feels like it has become part of my job function) and stood my ground regarding the parameters of my work.

Calling out someone's unprofessionally does not step outside of the professional framework, so why is it that when I flex my professional muscle, I'm met with insult? Because I have dared to live a life outside of the one prescribed as a person born male and succeeded, I am challenging the very core beliefs of a massive faction of society. In a desperate attempt to protect the status quo, this type of violence is used to nullify my success by reducing me to the failure this system positions me as.

Recently, during a domestic dispute between my parents, my stepfather asked my mother why she was quick to judge his son's drug addiction and not the fact that I was a "homosexual". She responded that the difference between us two was that my personal choices didn't impact her or anyone else negatively. While I was hurt by his insinuation that my sexual orientation was akin to drug addiction, I understood in grasping at straws, he couldn't find anything else to fault me on.

I wonder if perhaps this logic applies to the workplace discrimination I sometimes face. They may mean no harm by it, but for my colleagues to call out my sexual orientation during disputes makes me realise that we have not seen much of a shift in attitudes towards lesbian, gay, bisexual, transgender and intersex (LGBTI) people since discrimination based on sexual orientation was banned by our constitutional court. This kind of soft discrimination rears its head with every joke cracked; every comparison made on the basis of sexuality and even compliments attributing one's successes to their sexuality.

You may ask why I am so affected by something that seems trivial considering the violence met by LGBTI people in our townships, but I believe that we shouldn't be negotiating tolerance of intolerance. Slurs about one's sexuality impacts their confidence and productivity. A 2014 study by the Human Rights Campaign Foundation found that more than half of their sample of LGBTI employees hid who they were at work; one in four reported hearing negative comments such as "That's so gay" in the workplace; and one in five LGBTI workers reported looking for a new job specifically because their working environment wasn't very accepting of LGBTI identities.

Gender-based discrimination is rife in the workplace, and not only impacts affected persons at an individual level, but has structural consequences too: the lack of access to opportunities, unemployment... Early last year, a study by Ernesto Reuben of Columbia Business School asked test participants to hire candidates for a math task where both genders performed equally. It found participants were twice as likely to hire "the man" for the simple reason that they were seen as being better at math than women. This is despite the global trend where females are doing better at school than males – math included – according to the American Psychological Association. A review of the annual national assessment tests of 2012 in South Africa backs up these findings. Gender bias and stereotyping are not only unfounded, but damaging.

At a societal level, the impact of fear of discrimination is far more devastating as many LGBTI males' fear of judgment forces them to live heteronormative lives by day, while engaging in risky sexual behaviour with other men behind closed doors and in dark rooms of gay clubs. The South African National Aids Council believes that as many as 37% of men who sleep with men (MSM) are HIV positive – while the Johannesburg eThekwini Men's Study found that close to 50% of their sample of MSM tested positive. The average age of participants in the latter study was 22 years old – a faction often described as the backbone of our country's economic future.

While being Drama Queen of the Year is all fun and games, it doesn't become funny when my future employment is stifled because my reference jokingly mentions this momentous achievement. Call me crazy – actually don't – but shouldn't my achievements be the measure of competence?

THE PINK TONGUE (2015)

SIGMA OF LOVING SOMEONE WHO DIED OF AIDS-RELATED COMPLICATIONS

Chapter 56

I make it a point to tell anyone I date that I once had a partner that died of Aids-related complications. So many loved ones have lost their lives because of the stigma attached to HIV, and I refuse to enter into a relationship with someone who carries those prejudices.

The unfortunate reality is that, for many, I must have HIV by virtue of the fact that my partner of five years did. The idea alone is hard for them to deal with; my single status is testament to that.

The response I almost always get has become so predictable that I have prepared cues for the flood of questions that follow – as well as the eminent break-up texts:

"Yes, I did know he was HIV-positive. I loved him. That didn't matter to me."

"Don't feel bad. It was very hard to deal with when he died, but many years have passed and I am able to move forward."

"Of course, I have tested since then; I test every six months."

"Okay. I understand."

I do understand why they leave; HIV has devastated our community. Black men who have sex with men (MSM) account for 50% of all new HIV infections in the US and around 50% of all Black MSM in South Africa are HIV-positive. It is scary. But, you would think that we'd know better considering how prominent it is among us.

Instead, we continue to shy away from it as if it doesn't exist. Many of the men I've dated would not have given it a second thought if I had not brought it up in the first place. They feel like they've dodged a bullet, but the truth is that they are probably not going to have a conversation like that with the next person they are trying to get with.

The fear of HIV has scared so many people into silence. Guys don't ask questions, afraid of what they will hear; and others, too scared to disclose their positive status because they are not only afraid of rejection, but the social consequences that might follow the discovery of their secret.

A few years ago, the South African government conducted a study on the effect that stigma had on HIV and found that it had a profound impact on the number of new HIV infections and was the leading cause of Aids-related deaths.

People are so scared of what others will say that they'd rather not seek the sexual reproductive health services they need to stay healthy or medication they'd need to stay alive. They would rather die than be labeled HIV-positive, even the insinuation of it. And they have every reason to feel that way. Ostracisation is real – trust me, I know.

So, why would I put myself through all of this?

First of all, I will not disrespect the memory of a remarkable human being by acting as if they never existed. That man contributed too much to my life and to my development to be swept under any rug.

Secondly, I refuse to perpetuate a cycle that caused the death of someone I planned to grow old with. Why let someone else go through the pain I experienced because I selfishly want to fit in or be loved? The more I speak about it, hopefully, the more others do – even if it is just gossip, let them talk!

But, I think most importantly, I am looking for someone who will accept me with all of my baggage. I feel like that's a true sign of love or like, and of course maturity.

If someone is going to run for the hills because they think I might be sick, then by all means, let them. Because, if the final question they ask me isn't "When do we get tested together?" then we're just not in the same mental space anyways.

The Daily Vox (2018)

ACKNOWLEDGEMENTS

It was a random, sunny day that the idea to compile my thoughts into a book came to me on the steps of the Lincoln Memorial – the exact same spot where Dr Martin Luther King delivered his famous "I had a dream" speech. I was inspired that day to contemplate my own legacy in this world; and to make sense of everything I had already done until then, and everything that would come.

That moment will not have been possible without the pause the Fulbright Fellowship afforded me when I thought I had reached my professional peak. That random thought many never have materialised into an actual book had AfroStory not made it their mission to create access for thousands of authors like me. I am deeply grateful to both organisations and their commitment to cultivating talent across the African continent.

There are a multitude of organisations, writers and activists that have shaped my craft, knowledge and thinking over the past 17 years. I thank you, too. I am a better writer because of you. I am a better storyteller because of you. But, most of all, I am a better person because of you. You have all helped me understand my purpose, and instilled in me the confidence to believe that I can change the world in some way, for the better.

To my family and friends (and I have been blessed with so many) when the world didn't see my potential, you kept me motivated; and when it refused to acknowledge my humanity, you surrounded me with love. You are the only reason I survive this cruel world. You are the reason I want so badly to change it. My community. My tribe.

And last, and certainly not least, I have to acknowledge my mother. I get my strength from her, as well as my tenacity. She always saw in me the person I am today, and would not dare accept anything less. She did everything in her power to support me, on her own, and still does. Her selflessness inspires me.

ABOUT THE AUTHOR

Never one to shy away from any topic, Angelo C Louw has built a reputation on pushing the bar in public debate around racist relations in contemporary South Africa.

A journalist by profession and an activist at heart, his work has featured in hundreds publications around the world and has found its way into a plethora of academic writing. This Wits Journalism graduate focuses on the intricacies of race in our current socio-political climate, paying particular attention to minority groups that are often overlooked by mainstream media.

Louw's formidable media presence has helped shape our nation's reformative policies for well over a decade, earning him many accolades – including a Fulbright Fellowship at the University of Maryland, United States. Louw has served three editorships at magazines in South Africa and abroad, acquiring his first editor-in-chief title at the age of 25.

His critically acclaimed documentaries have traveled the world, and inspired change for some of South Africa's most vulnerable communities.

ABOUT THE BOOK

"The Problem with Black People" is a selection of writings by award-winning film-maker and social justice activist Angelo C Louw. Spanning his ten-year career as a columnist, this body of work unpacks the intricacies of race and race relations in contemporary South Africa through an intersectional lens.

The first-time author, whose journalistic focus lies in the mainstreaming voices from the margins of society, uses his debut book to redress misconceptions about race and inequality through fact, and not popular opinion.

This anthology advances an agenda seeking to reclaim narratives of people of colour which are systemically destructive and stifling to their communities; turning the cliché on its head.

By setting the record straight, Louw aims to enlighten, as well as empower. *"The Problem With Black People"* explores themes of climate justice, socio-economic rights, public policy, youth, sex and sexuality, and HIV.

www.ingramcontent.com/pod-product-compliance
Lightning Source LLC
Chambersburg PA
CBHW070947250726
48663CB00002B/116